People to Know

Ernest Hemingway

Writer and Adventurer

Della A. Yannuzzi

Dedicated to my sister, Marion Groe

Library of Congress Cataloging-in-Publication Data

Yannuzzi, Della A.
Ernest Hemingway : writer and adventurer / Della A. Yannuzzi.
p. cm.
Includes bibliographical references and index.
Summary: Describes the life and career of the Pulitzer and Nobel prize winner whose accounts of his adventures and new style of writing brought him worldwide recognition.
ISBN 0-89490-979-7
1. Hemingway, Ernest, 1899-1961—Juvenile literature. 2. Authors, American—20th century—Biography—Juvenile literature.
3. Adventure and adventurers—United States—Biography—Juvenile literature.
[1. Hemingway, Ernest, 1899–1961. 2. Authors, American.] I. Title.
PS3515.E37Z9815 1998
813'.52—dc21
[b] 97-33351
CIP
AC

Printed in the United States of America

10 9 8 7 6 5 4 3 2 1

Illustration Credits: Courtesy of the Ernest Hemingway Collection, John Fitzgerald Kennedy Library, pp. 4, 8, 13, 15, 18, 21, 25, 28, 36, 41, 46, 52, 55, 61, 69, 72, 82, 93; Special Collections and Archives, Knox College Library, Galesburg, Illinois, p. 87.

Cover Illustration: Courtesy of the Ernest Hemingway Collection, John Fitzgerald Kennedy Library.

Contents

Ernest Hemingway

1

An American Legend

In 1940, when Ernest Hemingway did not win the Pulitzer Prize in Literature for his popular novel *For Whom the Bell Tolls*, a newspaper reporter quoted him as saying: "If I'd won that prize, I'd think I was slipping. I've been writing for twenty years and I never have won a prize. I've gotten along all right."[1]

In the next ten years, Hemingway did not have another book published, although he was contributing many articles to *Collier's* magazine. Then in 1950, *Across the River and into the Trees* was published. This book did not receive good reviews, and many critics and readers wondered whether Ernest Hemingway's talent was slipping.[2] Then, in 1952,

Hemingway wrote a short novel called *The Old Man and the Sea.* A year later it was awarded the Pulitzer Prize in Literature. This award helped to reestablish Hemingway's reputation as one of America's greatest writers.

Where did the idea for *The Old Man and the Sea* come from? There are many thoughts on this, and literary scholars debate whether one real incident inspired Hemingway to create his most popular story. In 1936, Hemingway had written in *Esquire* magazine about the thrill and excitement of deep-sea fishing. He told the story of an old man who had caught a gigantic marlin, only to lose his prized catch to a shark.[3] More recently, a reporter spoke with Gregorio Fuentes, who was Hemingway's boat captain on the *Pilar* as they traveled in the Caribbean waters. Fuentes, age ninety-six when he was interviewed, described the incident that he believed was the catalyst for *The Old Man and the Sea*: One day, Hemingway and his wife Mary were on the *Pilar* with Captain Fuentes. While traveling in the Gulf Stream along Cuba's northern coast, they came upon an old man and a boy fishing in a small boat. The old man was struggling with a big marlin at the end of his fishing line. The fish, in turn, was being chased by hungry sharks. Hemingway offered to help the old man, but he was told to go away. Instead, the *Pilar* came up alongside the small boat and Hemingway tossed some snacks and drinks to the man and the boy. The *Pilar* stayed nearby for a while to see what would happen. Hemingway watched them for a long time, but he left before finding out whether the old man brought his fish home safely. Later he learned that the old man had died.[4]

There may be debate about the true inspiration for *The Old Man and the Sea*, but it is clear that all Hemingway needed to create his Pulitzer Prize–winning novel was his love of the sea and a good imagination. The book tells the story of an old fisherman named Santiago, his young friend Manolin, and the fisherman's desire to bring home a large fish that will feed many people. During his struggle with a great marlin, many thoughts swirl through Santiago's mind:

> *"The fish is my friend too," he said aloud. "I have never seen or heard of such a fish. But I must kill him." . . . Then he was sorry for the great fish that had nothing to eat and his determination to kill him never relaxed in his sorrow for him. How many people will he feed, he thought. But are they worthy to eat him? . . . I do not understand these things, he thought.*[5]

The story of a simple, hardworking man and his battle with a great fish touched the hearts of many people. Hemingway explored the ideas of courage, respect, honor, loyalty, friendship, and loss.

The Old Man and the Sea once again established Hemingway's reputation as a great American writer. His new creative energy at the mature age of fifty-five had produced a small masterpiece. The novella was first published in the September 1, 1952, issue of *Life* magazine. The magazine sold more than five million copies in two days. A week later, Hemingway's

The Old Man and the Sea *reestablished Hemingway's reputation as an American literary giant.*

publisher, Charles Scribner's Sons, released the book. It became an instant best-seller.

The success of his new book proved to readers and critics that Hemingway was still worthy of his stature and reputation as a great twentieth-century writer. Today, Hemingway's most popular book has been translated into several different languages and continues to earn money for Hemingway's heirs.

Hemingway once told a friend, "The worst death for anyone is to lose the center of his being, the thing he really is. . . . to retire from what you do—and what you do makes you what you are—is to back up into the grave."[6] For Hemingway, that thing was being a writer. The American legend he had created for himself was much larger than he could have imagined. He had been honored with a distinguished writing award, had led a creative and often dangerous life, married four times and had three sons, and had earned the admiration of many people. He once confided to his brother that "the true story of a man's life should really cover everything that happened to him and around him every twenty-four hours for fifty years."[7]

That would be impossible for anyone, but especially so for Ernest Hemingway, who had lived life to the fullest, both personally and professionally.

2

Life in Oak Park, Illinois

Ernest Miller Hemingway was born on July 21, 1899, in Oak Park, Illinois, to Grace and Clarence Edmunds Hemingway. He came into the world in the second-floor bedroom of his maternal grandfather's house, delivered by his own father, who was a physician. Ernest was the second child and first son, following his sister Marcelline, born eighteen months earlier. In 1902, his sister Ursula was born, followed by Madelaine ("Sunny") in 1904, and Carol in 1911. In 1915, when Ernest was sixteen years old, his brother, Leicester, was born. Ernest soon nicknamed him Lester de Pester, and later called him The Baron.

Ernest and his sister Marcelline were close in age,

and Grace Hemingway, like many other mothers at that time, began to dress them alike, referring to them as her "twins."[1] Even though he was a boy, she put both Ernest and his sister in dresses and hats. Her choice of dress for Ernest caused him to rebel. As he grew older, Ernest began to show what a tough little boy he was by playing soldier games. When he was asked what he was afraid of, he exclaimed, " 'fraid of nothing!"[2]

Grace Hemingway was devoted to her six children. She started albums for each of them that covered the years from their births to age eighteen. She also tried to spend individual time with each of them. She often took the children to theaters and museums. She was gifted musically and wanted her children to have an appreciation of music. She encouraged all of them to play musical instruments. Ernest took cello lessons, Marcelline played the violin, and Sunny studied harp.

Ernest's mother had come close to having a career as an opera singer. Unfortunately, she had poor vision due to a case of scarlet fever as a child. The glare of the stage lights bothered her eyes. She decided against a singing career, and soon married her neighbor.

Ernest's father, known as Ed, was quite different from the outspoken, take-charge woman he had married. Ed Hemingway was quiet, thoughtful, moody, and sometimes short-tempered. He preferred the simple things in life. He liked to cook and prepare meals. He also enjoyed canning fruits and vegetables. His wife, on the other hand, was outgoing, enjoyed entertaining at home, and liked the finer things in life. The two opposing personalities of Ernest's parents produced problems in their family.

Grace and Ed Hemingway had trouble agreeing in two areas: how to raise their children and how to manage their family finances. Ed Hemingway was a strict parent who had certain rules that he wanted his children to obey. One rule was that on Sundays they could not play or visit friends. His wife agreed with him on some things, but she wanted a more relaxed attitude so her children could enjoy life.

Grace Hemingway was the organizer and planner in the family, but sometimes her plans were too ambitious and costly. There were often arguments between the Hemingways concerning her spending habits, even though she contributed to the family's income by giving music and voice lessons.

Ernest and his father formed a strong bond in a household filled with women. In addition to being a physician, Ernest's father was an outdoorsman with a passion for nature, hunting, and fishing. Until Ernest was nine years old, he and his family lived in his maternal grandfather's house in Oak Park, but their summers were spent at Walloon Lake in northern Michigan on land that the Hemingways had bought in 1899. Later, they built a cottage on this land. Grace Hemingway named it Windemere, after a famous lake in England. Ernest made his first trip to the Michigan woodlands only weeks after his birth. By the age of two, he was fishing with his father, and at age three he had his own fishing rod. When Ernest was about six years old, his parents bought a farm across the lake and named it Longfield Farm.

Five-year-old Ernest Hemingway was already a serious fisherman.

For the next seventeen years, Ernest spent his summers at Windemere, where he was allowed the freedom to roam the woods, fish in the lake, and hunt birds and small game. He also liked to swim in the cool, spring-fed waters of Walloon Lake and listen to stories told by the Ottawa Indians, who lived nearby. Summers were free and lazy and open to the imagination, but the Hemingway children still had to do chores at Windemere or at Longfield Farm. There was always wood to be chopped, apples to be picked, or fish to be caught for an evening's meal.

In his teens, Ernest became close friends with Bill and Katy Smith, neighboring youngsters who lived at Horton Bay, a few miles from Windemere. Katy developed a crush on Ernest, but their friendship never became anything more. Years later, she was responsible for introducing him to his first wife, and later on she married one of Ernest's friends, the writer John Dos Passos.

Ernest acquired his love of the outdoors from his summers spent in Michigan, and he began to develop his talent for writing during this time. Often he would disappear into the woods with paper and pen and let his imagination run wild. Later, he set many of his short stories in the Michigan woods or in outdoor settings with a main character named Nick Adams. It appeared that Ernest was acquiring important insights and traits from both his parents. A love of nature and the outdoors came from his father, and a love of words, books, and art from his mother.[3]

In 1905, Ernest's maternal grandfather died, leaving a sizable inheritance to Grace Hemingway. She decided

Grace Hemingway caught a big fish in Walloon Lake on an outing with Ernest, Ursula, and Marcelline in 1904.

to have a new house built, using the money her father had left to her. She chose a corner lot on Kenilworth Avenue and Iowa Street, not far from her father's house. It was a short walk to the Oak Park Public Library, where Ernest spent many hours.

Ernest's mother was very specific about the type of house she wanted. There should be medical offices for her husband, but they must be separate from the main house. Next, there would have to be a large kitchen with lots of cabinets and working space, eight bedrooms, and a living room. There would also be a large music room with a fifteen-foot ceiling and a balcony the length of the room—thirty feet long. Her plan was to hold music recitals and concerts in the large room, as well as to teach voice and piano. Later on, in high school, Ernest would find his own use for the music room when he decided to hold boxing matches on the highly polished wooden floors. His mother was unaware of these matches, of course.

Ernest's young years flew by quickly. He was kept busy with family life, music lessons, school, reading, and summer trips to Windemere. At the age of fourteen, he entered Oak Park High School. He did well in his studies, especially English, because he was drawn to writing. He contributed many articles to the high school newspaper, the *Trapeze*, and wrote poetry and short stories that were published in the *Literary Tabula*, the school literary magazine. His first short story, "Judgment of Manitou," was published in the February 1916 issue of the *Literary Tabula*. The following excerpt from "Judgment of

Manitou" shows the promise of a talented writer already developing his writing style:

> *Suddenly, as Dick entered a growth of spruce, he was jerked off his feet, high into the air. When his head had cleared from the bang it had received by striking the icy crust, he saw that he was suspended in the air by a rope which was attached to a spruce tree, which had been bent over to form the spring for a snare, such as is used to capture rabbits. His fingers barely touched the crust, and as he struggled and the cord grew tighter on his lead he saw what he had sensed to be following him. Slowly out of the woods trotted a band of gaunt, white, hungry timber wolves, and squatted on their haunches in a circle round him.*[4]

He tried out for sports, but he seemed too clumsy and small for football and swimming. He was also interested in boxing and begged his father for lessons. The result of his first boxing lesson was a broken nose, but he didn't quit. The next day he was back at the gym. By the age of fifteen, Ernest finally began to grow tall. He went from five feet four inches to six feet tall.

Also during his high school years, Ernest gave himself the nickname of Hemingstein, the first of many that he used throughout his life. He would give nicknames to friends, family, girlfriends, wives, and children.

As Ernest grew older, his trips to Walloon Lake became a combination of fun and work. He and his father worked out an arrangement for Ernest to do necessary chores such as chopping wood, harvesting

Grace Hemingway had strong opinions about the design of the family's new house, built in 1906 in Oak Park.

vegetables, picking fruit in the Longfield Farm orchards, and making repairs on the cottage. Even with all this work, he still had plenty of time to read, explore the woods, write in his journal, and get into trouble.

Once, when Ernest was sixteen years old, he shot a blue heron, which was a protected species. He left it in a boat while he went ashore to have something to eat. The heron was discovered by the local game warden's son, who confronted Ernest. He denied shooting the bird. When the game warden himself came looking for Ernest at Windemere, Grace Hemingway ordered the warden to get off her property. Ernest sneaked off to his Uncle George's home in nearby Ironton. Finally, Ernest's father suggested that his son swallow his pride, plead guilty, and pay the fine. Ernest eventually returned home. He had to pay a fifteen-dollar fine and listen to a lecture from the judge.[5]

When high school graduation time arrived, Ernest knew what he wanted to do: enlist in the Army and then become a writer. But his parents had their own ideas about their son's future. They wanted him to go to college, and they refused to give their permission for Ernest to enlist. For the time being, Ernest put aside his plans for military service and concentrated on becoming a writer.[6]

3

Work, War, and Love

After graduation from Oak Park High in 1917, Hemingway was certain he wanted to make his living as a writer, but he had no definite plans. His parents were still trying to persuade him to go to Oberlin College, where his sister Marcelline was already in her second year. Hemingway resisted their pleas, and eventually his father gave in and wrote a letter to his brother Tyler in Kansas City. He asked if Tyler could help Ernest get a newspaper job. Tyler Hemingway knew Henry J. Haskell, chief editorial writer at *The Kansas City Star*, and soon Hemingway was offered a job as a cub reporter for the newspaper. The position, however, was not available until October. In the meantime, the

The Hemingway children gather for a snapshot (from top): Marcelline, Ernest, Ursula, Madelaine, Carol, and Leicester.

aspiring young writer decided to spend the summer at Windemere. Hemingway helped out around Longfield Farm, took fishing trips, visited with friends, and wrote short stories, based mostly on people and places he knew.

Even at this early age, Hemingway was establishing a pattern of writing about people and places he knew and loved, or sometimes about people he didn't particularly like. His characters and stories were supposedly fictional, but there was always some person who thought he or she had been a model for one of his characters. In the years ahead, Hemingway would continue to blend fact and fiction into his work. Many times, he angered and hurt people who were certain the author had described them unflatteringly in a short story or novel.

As much as Hemingway loved Walloon Lake and the Michigan woods, he was eager to be out on his own, away from the watchful eyes of his mother and father. He was looking forward to going to Kansas City in the fall of 1917. When the time came, Hemingway left for Kansas City and moved in with Carl Edgar, a friend of Katy Smith's. Hemingway was a sociable man, and soon he had a network of friends that included writers and news reporters.[1]

The young Hemingway was also a quick learner. He listened and learned from more seasoned reporters and picked up tips from them. One writer, a reporter named Lionel Moise, had a terrific memory for stories and could write them fast and accurately. Hemingway worked hard at his job. Although he earned only fifteen dollars a week, he gained excellent experience. He learned how to write simply, clearly, and in short, crisp sentences. Many of his first published short stories came out of his experience at *The Kansas City Star*.

Hemingway also displayed a talent for getting the inside scoop. He had a pleasant personality and could often talk his way into action-packed situations. The stories he liked to cover were those he found at the police stations, hospitals, and railroad station. Wherever the action was, that's where the young reporter wanted to be. Working in Kansas City was an eye-opener for the young man from the quiet and proper Victorian town of Oak Park, Illinois. This new experience was fine with Hemingway because he was always looking for new adventures.

Hemingway had not forgotten about his original plan to join the armed services. Now that he was older, he decided to apply. However, he had poor vision in his left eye, and this prevented him from enlisting. Still, Hemingway was determined to go overseas. When another reporter, Ted Brumback, who had lost an eye in college, told him that he had driven an ambulance overseas in the American Field Service and was going to reenlist, Hemingway decided to do the same. On April 6, 1917, the United States had entered into World War I against Germany. By the end of April, Hemingway left his job at the newspaper, after working there for only seven months.

Both Brumback and Hemingway volunteered for overseas duty with the American Red Cross. Hemingway passed the physical exam, but the doctor suggested he start wearing eyeglasses. The young ex-reporter did not take the doctor's advice because he disliked the idea of wearing glasses at the age of eighteen. Hemingway was thirty-one when he finally decided to wear glasses.[2]

In May 1918, Hemingway departed for Europe as a commissioned second lieutenant in the Red Cross. He was assigned first to Bordeaux, France, then to Milan, Italy. Hemingway was kept busy with his duties as an ambulance driver. He was stationed in the town of Schio and assigned to drive a tall Fiat ambulance truck up into the mountains. His job was to pick up wounded soldiers and bring them back down for treatment. The work was tedious, but that didn't bother Hemingway as much as being away from the action: "I'm going to get out of this ambulance section and see if I can't find where the war is."[3]

Hemingway volunteered to deliver coffee, candy, and other items to soldiers at the front lines near the village of Fossalta, near the Piave River. He rode a bicycle to get to the front lines, along the lower Piave. Unfortunately, on July 8, not long after he was assigned to this area, he was seriously injured by a mortar shell. The shell exploded a few feet from him, sending pieces of shrapnel into Hemingway's legs and knees. Hemingway wrote later that although he was gravely injured, he managed to carry another wounded soldier on his back to safety before losing consciousness. For this act of bravery, he was recommended for the Italian Silver Medal of Valor and the War Cross of Merit.[4]

Hemingway was transported to a makeshift hospital in Milan. The building was a stone mansion with

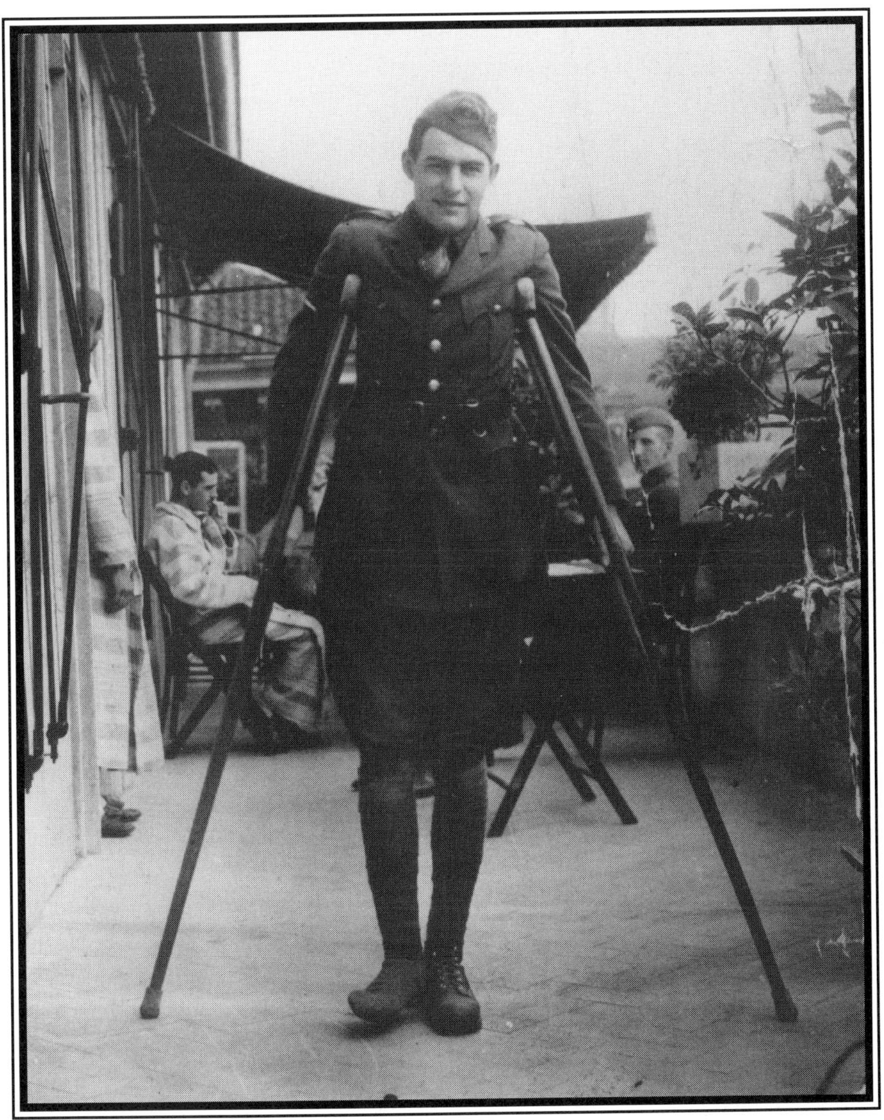

Ernest Hemingway, wounded in 1918 during World War I, was sent to a hospital in Milan to recuperate.

balconies and striped awnings, lush green plants, flower boxes, and wicker chairs. It was here that Hemingway met Agnes Hannah von Kurowsky, a twenty-six-year-old American nurse. Von Kurowsky was attracted to the good-looking eighteen-year-old from Oak Park. Hemingway appeared infatuated with the attractive older nurse.

It did not take long for Hemingway to declare his love for von Kurowsky, who had been raised in Washington, D.C. She returned Hemingway's feelings, although she realized the two of them were still in the middle of a war and nothing was certain.[5] Hemingway wrote letters home saying that he had fallen in love with a pretty nurse. When he was well enough to travel, he left the hospital for some well-earned leave, and von Kurowsky was reassigned to Florence. They promised to write to each other, and they did, sometimes twice a day. Eventually, they were able to see each other before Hemingway left for the United States. His hopes were that von Kurowsky would follow him later on, after he had found a job. Then he would marry her. These were Hemingway's plans when he returned to Oak Park to convalesce.

By January 1919, Hemingway was back in his parents' house, a celebrated hero to his family, friends, and strangers. He was interviewed by local newspapers and invited to give talks to women's clubs and other civic groups. Each time, his war stories seemed to grow and grow and grow. There was no doubt that he had suffered severe injuries, but the retelling of his heroic actions became more and more dramatic.

Hemingway continued to write to von Kurowsky, making all sorts of plans for their future together. She answered his letters, but then a letter arrived from her that devastated Hemingway. She told him she had met another man, an Italian officer from a noble Italian family. They had become engaged and she said that her relationship with Hemingway had been a "wonderful friendship," but that for her it was not love.[6] Hemingway did not take this news well. He refused to eat or leave his third-floor bedroom. There is no doubt that the American nurse was Hemingway's first true love. Years later, she would become the model for Catherine Barkley, a central character in his novel *A Farewell to Arms*.

This period of Hemingway's life made him grow up quickly. Witnessing the devastation of war, suffering serious injuries, falling in love with a woman and then losing her left memories that the young Hemingway would never be able to forget. These life experiences would later be expressed in his writing. The themes of courage in the face of adversity, loss of love, war, death, and honor would become important ideas in his work. But for the time being, he was still a nineteen-year-old living in his parents' home.

Hemingway spent that summer at Walloon Lake in Michigan. He fished, read, wrote, and visited old friends. He took a long fishing trip with two friends into the woods of Michigan. In the future he would write a short story based on this experience. It was called "Big Two-Hearted River" and featured Nick Adams.

The first months of celebrity status were finally

Hospital nurse Agnes von Kurowsky was Ernest Hemingway's first true love. Years later, she appeared as Catherine Barkley in his novel A Farewell to Arms.

slipping away. Hemingway was moody, unsure of his future, and still living with the physical and emotional effects of the war. When his family returned to Oak Park at the end of the summer, Hemingway stayed behind to work on his writing. He was sending out stories to *Redbook* and the *Saturday Evening Post*, but they were being sent back with rejection slips.

Finally, in late fall 1919, Hemingway's luck changed. He had met a successful Canadian businessman named Ralph Connable, who needed someone to tutor his son Ralph back home in Toronto. Hemingway told Connable about his writing, and Connable introduced him to the features editor of the *Toronto Star*. Hemingway sold more than twenty articles to the newspaper's Saturday edition, the *Star Weekly*.

Hemingway lived with the Connables from January until late May of 1920 and then returned to Michigan for more fishing and writing. His relationship with his parents had become increasingly strained. Family tensions reached a peak that summer, when Hemingway's mother made her annual trip to Windemere.

On July 21, 1920, Hemingway was going to be twenty-one years old. He was still writing and trying to perfect his craft. He considered writing to be his life's work, although it was not well-paying work. His parents felt that since he was unemployed he should help out around the summer home, but Hemingway had his own ideas. He rebelled at helping out with the chores and instead spent time with his friends at a nearby small village called Horton Bay. He was usually gone for many hours and showed up at home only for his meals. Since his father could not stay at Windemere for the entire summer, the task of dealing with Ernest's idleness fell upon his mother. She complained in letters to her husband that Ernest was not helping out with the farm or household chores. Ernest's father decided to write to his son. In his letter, he urged Ernest to settle down, get a respectable job, and help his mother around the summerhouse. Instead, Hemingway continued to stay away.[7]

Unfortunately, Hemingway and his mother never really understood each other. She saw his rebellious nature as irresponsible while, in truth, he was attempting to break loose from parental ties. Everything came to a climax the night Hemingway and his friend Ted accompanied Hemingway's sisters Ursula and Sunny, along with some of their friends from a nearby cottage, on a secret nighttime picnic. When the friends' mother found that her teenage daughters were not in their beds, she went to Windemere. Grace Hemingway soon discovered that her son and two daughters were also missing.

Hemingway and his sisters arrived home in the early morning hours and found the two mothers waiting for them. Grace Hemingway immediately grounded her daughters and told her son and his friend to go to Horton Bay for a while. The picnic had been a harmless affair, but Hemingway's mother saw it as the ultimate act of irresponsibility on the part of her son. Hemingway's father also agreed that Ernest had gone too far this time.

Although Grace Hemingway was angry with her son, she still kept her plans for his twenty-first birthday dinner. Hemingway showed up, but there was little peace. In the days following the picnic trouble, Hemingway's mother gave her son a long letter listing her complaints and telling him to grow up and be a responsible young man. She wrote that "a mother's love seems to me like a bank. . . . You have overdrawn."[8] She also told him he was no longer welcome at Windemere until he improved his behavior. Ed Hemingway agreed that their son had been showing a lack of respect and love toward both of them. It was time Ernest got his life in order.

Perhaps Hemingway needed this abrupt break from his parents to move on with his life and his writing. However, the manner in which he was ordered from the family summer home was something he could never forget. He now had to find another place to live, and he had to get a paying job to support himself. He stayed in a boardinghouse in Boyne City and earned money doing odd jobs. Then he moved to Chicago and lived with friends. He confided to a friend that after his parents told him to leave, he saw himself as "literally homeless, kicked out for no good reason."[9]

4

Hadley and Paris

Hemingway could not have imagined how much his life would change after his move to Chicago. He knew there would be new experiences, but falling in love again with an older woman was a pleasant and unexpected surprise.

The woman who became the object of Hemingway's affection was Hadley Elizabeth Richardson, an attractive twenty-nine-year-old with red hair and light blue eyes. She was a quiet woman who had musical talent and found comfort and pleasure in playing the piano. She was from a well-to-do family in St. Louis, Missouri, and was the youngest of four children—two other girls and a boy.

Richardson's later school years had been spent at

the Mary Institute, a private school in St. Louis, where she met Katy Smith, Hemingway's old friend from Michigan. After graduating, Richardson enrolled at Bryn Mawr College for one year, but the stress of college work and the death of her oldest sister, Dorothea, forced her to give up her studies.

In 1920, Richardson's mother died. Until her mother's death, Richardson had lived a tightly structured and secluded life. Now, when she received an invitation to visit her friend Katy Smith in Chicago, Richardson quickly accepted. Smith asked her brother Kenley and his wife, Dolores, to let Richardson stay in their apartment.

When Hemingway first saw Richardson at the Smith's apartment in late October 1920, he knew the woman with the golden red hair, blue serge dress, and light blue eyes was the one for him. She was also attracted to the young man with the charming smile who went by the nicknames of Hemingstein, Wemedge, and Nesto. Richardson added her own nicknames for him, calling him Tatie or Tiny.

Richardson was flattered by the interest and attention the twenty-one-year-old writer was showing her.[1] She was drawn to his outgoing personality, boyish charm, and intense brown eyes. Richardson was quiet, passive, and unsure of herself. Hemingway, on the other hand, was outspoken and confident that he would one day be a successful published writer. They were very different from each other, but there were also similarities. They both had midwestern backgrounds, enjoyed the outdoors, and liked to read. Most important, they enjoyed each other's company and had long conversations about their families and Hemingway's plans to become a writer.

Richardson's visit lasted for three weeks. During this time, the couple spent many hours together. They parted, promising to write. They decided to wait to see whether their relationship would develop into anything more permanent. They wrote many letters to each other. In fact, their relationship developed through their letters. Hemingway even sent his stories in the mail for her to review. Then, in December 1920, Richardson had another chance to visit Chicago and made plans to see Hemingway. Once again, they got along well, learning more about each other through their long talks.

Hemingway was already praising Richardson's qualities to friends and in letters to his mother. He wanted to marry her in spite of some friends' advice that he was too young to get tied down. In March, the young writer went to St. Louis to visit Richardson and meet her sister Fonnie. Richardson's sister took Hemingway aside and told him that Hadley would not make a good wife because she was weak and lazy.[2] She also thought that Hemingway was too young for her sister and that he would not be able to support her on a writer's salary. Of course, Hemingway didn't believe her. As for being young, well, he couldn't do anything about the age difference, but he did find a job as a writer for a magazine called *The Cooperative Commonwealth*. The job paid only forty dollars a week, but it was a start in the right direction. He also earned extra money as a sparring partner at a gym.

Hemingway and Richardson's love for each other continued to grow. She encouraged him in his writing, and he was opening up a whole new world for her. She once said that being near him "removes every fear and worry."[3] They were making plans for an exciting life together. To show her support for his work, she presented Hemingway with a Corona typewriter for his twenty-second birthday.

In the spring of 1921, the couple began to talk seriously about marriage. Hemingway knew it was time to bring his future wife to Oak Park to meet his parents and to announce their intentions. The Hemingways liked Richardson immediately, and Grace Hemingway, in particular, was pleased that her son had found a woman who was mature and who was a talented musician as well. As an expression of goodwill, Hemingway's mother offered them the use of the Windemere cottage for their honeymoon.

The wedding date was set for September 3, 1921, at a country church in Horton Bay, Michigan. Richardson wore an ankle-length ivory lace dress, satin slippers, a long veil, and a wreath of flowers around her red hair. She carried a bouquet of baby's breath in her arms. Hemingway wore a white shirt, striped tie, dark vest and jacket, and white trousers. Leicester Hemingway remembers his older brother as being nervous ("His heavy white trousers seemed to have a serious case of the shiver"), but after the marriage ceremony, he seemed to be fine.[4]

After the honeymoon at Windemere, Hemingway and his wife set up housekeeping in a dreary fifth-floor

On their wedding day in 1921, Hadley Richardson and Ernest Hemingway pose with his parents and some of his siblings. From left to right are Carol, Marcelline, Hadley, Ernest, Grace, Leicester, and Clarence ("Ed") Hemingway.

walk-up apartment on North Dearborn Street in Chicago. Money was tight, but they decided they could manage if they lived frugally. Hemingway contributed to their finances through writing jobs and whatever stories he sold, but their main support came from an annual $3,000 trust fund that had been set up for his wife. This arrangement was fine with the new Mrs. Hemingway, who viewed her financial contribution as an investment in her husband's future as a writer.

Unfortunately, Hemingway was not having much luck selling his short stories. He wanted to write novels, but the long hours at his magazine job took away precious time from his own writing. Finally, he decided to leave the job because he was eager to work on his own fiction. His luck started to change the day he and his wife had dinner with Sherwood Anderson, a writer who had spent some time in Paris. Hemingway told Anderson that he was thinking of going to Italy, where the cost of living was cheaper. Anderson suggested that Paris was a better place for writers and artists because it was a literary and creative city that offered a nurturing atmosphere for struggling young people. He even offered to write letters of introduction to American writers living there, such as Gertrude Stein, Ezra Pound, and Sylvia Beach, owner of a bookshop called Shakespeare and Company. Hemingway took Anderson's advice and made arrangements with the *Toronto Star* newspaper in Canada to work as a foreign correspondent in Europe. His salary was only $75 a week plus expenses, but his wife had also inherited $8,000 from an uncle. For the time being, the Hemingways had enough money to support themselves.

In early December, Hemingway and his wife left for Europe on an ocean liner called the *Leopoldina*. It was a cold, ten-day trip, but the Hemingways socialized with the other passengers and generally enjoyed themselves. Hadley Hemingway entertained the travelers by playing the piano, while Ernest entertained himself and others by sparring with a middleweight fighter who was heading for some boxing matches in Paris.

The Hemingways reached Le Havre, France, on December 22, 1921, and then took an evening train to Paris. They temporarily settled into the Hotel Jacob while they looked for an inexpensive apartment. Two weeks later, they found a fourth-floor walk-up at 74 rue de Cardinal Lemoine, which was located in a working-class district. The apartment had a kitchen with table and chairs and a two-burner gas stove. The bedroom had a large gilt-decorated mahogany bed with a good mattress. There was also a small fireplace that burned egg-shaped lumps of coal dust called *boulets*. A small closet was used as a bathroom. A chamber pot was provided on each floor of the winding staircase. Although the apartment was small, Hadley Hemingway managed to find space for a small rented piano. They hired a woman named Marie to help carry buckets of water upstairs, to clean the apartment, and to cook for them.

The biggest drawback to the apartment was the noisy dance hall in the building next door. Hemingway needed quiet and privacy to concentrate on his writing.

He rented a bedroom on the top floor of a hotel on the rue Mouffetard. Each morning, he walked past the cafés and sights and smells of Paris as he headed to his work. He wrote on a table in the small room that was kept warm by the heat of a fireplace. When he needed a break, he would snack on fruit and chestnuts, and then continue with his work. His goal, as he later recalled in his memoir *A Moveable Feast*, was to write "one true sentence" in his blue notebook, and then he could go on.[5]

Hemingway's style, or the style he was trying to develop, was that of writing in clear sentences without explaining or overstating too much. He liked to imply emotion, instead of bluntly stating it, and he would rewrite for hours to show the feelings of a story and its characters through their actions and thoughts. He also believed in luck and thought having a little of it in his writing could not hurt. "For luck you carried a horse chestnut and a rabbit's foot in your right pocket," he later wrote.[6]

In *A Moveable Feast*, he described his time as a writer in Paris: "It was wonderful to walk down the long flights of stairs knowing that I'd had good luck working. I always worked until I had something done and I always stopped when I knew what was going to happen next. That way I could be sure of going on the next day."[7]

After Hemingway finished his daily writing session, he would wander around the Parisian streets, and then stop to have lunch at a sidewalk café. Then, perhaps, he would continue his walk through the

Luxembourg Gardens or visit the Louvre art museum, where he admired the works of Edouard Manet, Paul Cezanne, Henri Matisse, and Claude Monet. On other occasions he might visit Gertrude Stein, a writer and art collector, whom he and his wife had met in March. Stein, forty-eight years old, and her companion Alice B. Toklas lived in a spacious studio apartment. Their home had become a meeting place for writers and artists. Stein owned paintings by Monet, Picasso, Braque, and other talented artists. She gave advice to Hemingway on which artists' work he should buy when he was able to afford it. She also agreed to look at some of his short stories, which she liked because they were written in clear, strong language.

Hemingway met many interesting people in Paris, including the writers James Joyce, F. Scott Fitzgerald, and Ezra Pound, whom he had met briefly while in Italy. Another person who came into Hemingway's life was Sylvia Beach. She had turned her Shakespeare and Company bookstore into a writer's haven. Beach was supportive of struggling writers and helped them in any way she could. She played an important role in helping James Joyce get his major work, *Ulysses*, published in the United States.

Shakespeare and Company also had a rental library where patrons could borrow books. Beach was especially sympathetic to writers who did not have the deposit money required to borrow books. Usually, she would trust them and lend the books without the deposit. She did this with Hemingway one day when he didn't have any money with him. Hemingway liked

As a young man in Paris, Hemingway began to develop the clear, crisp writing style that would make him famous.

Sylvia Beach and enjoyed browsing through the bookshelves of Shakespeare and Company.

During his Paris Period, Hemingway was also traveling on writing assignments to Switzerland, Turkey, Italy, and many other places. His wife stayed behind in Paris, often feeling lonely. These separations from her husband were their first since their marriage seven months earlier. However, the Hemingways had other opportunities to spend time together on their own trips around the city and countryside. They met with new friends, ate at good but inexpensive cafés, and took skiing, fishing, and hiking trips in Switzerland and Germany. Life was good for the young couple. Hemingway was developing his writing skills, earning some money from newspaper assignments, and seeing other parts of the world. Most important, he had the love and support of a wife who considered his writing worthwhile. But it was Hadley Hemingway's life that was especially enriched by her marriage to the aspiring writer. Her young husband's zest for life opened up her eyes to a world that had not existed for her in St. Louis. She blossomed into a happy, adventuresome young woman who was experiencing life the way Ernest Hemingway saw it: life that was lived to the fullest.

Hemingway summed up his feelings about Paris in this way. "If you are lucky enough to have lived in Paris as a young man, then wherever you go for the rest of your life, it stays with you, for Paris is a moveable feast."[8]

Unfortunately, there were also some unpleasant occurrences in Paris. One of the biggest upsets was the time Hemingway's manuscripts were stolen at a railroad station. In 1922, Hadley Hemingway was getting ready to meet her husband for a skiing trip to Switzerland. She decided to pack all of his handwritten and typed manuscripts, except for two short stories and some poetry that were elsewhere. She thought that he would want to work on them while they were vacationing. A porter had put her bag and the small case carrying the manuscripts on a baggage rack near her train seat. Her personal bag was up higher, and the smaller one lower down. She left the train briefly to buy a newspaper and returned to find the smaller bag missing. She was frantic when she discovered that it was gone.[9]

Hemingway tried to console his wife by telling her everything would be all right, but she felt that he was truly angry at her and would never forgive her. The loss of these manuscripts was something she was never able to forget. Hemingway was also distressed, but he began to work on more stories. The manuscripts were gone, and there was nothing to be done about them.

During the early 1920s, Hemingway's work was being published in small literary magazines, such as the *Transatlantic Review* and *The Little Review*. He was also working on a book called *Three Stories and Ten Poems*, which he dedicated to his wife, and another book called *In Our Time*. The first book was published in July 1923, in a small edition of three hundred copies.

In the middle of this literary success, Hadley Hemingway found she was pregnant with their first child. The Hemingways were excited about the news and decided to move to Toronto, Canada, to await the birth of their baby. Hemingway was already working for the *Toronto Star* as a foreign correspondent, and he made arrangements to work as a reporter for the newspaper's office in Canada. He wanted to have a regular income for the baby's needs, instead of the occasional magazine assignment he was getting while living in Paris. In August 1923, the Hemingways left Paris. They found an apartment in Toronto and tried to settle into their new routine. Hemingway went to work and his wife stayed at home.

Unfortunately, Hemingway worked for an assistant editor who did not particularly like him. He was given assignment after assignment that required long hours. Many of the assignments were out of town, and on a moment's notice the young writer had to pack his bags and leave his wife alone while he chased news stories.[10] Both Hemingways missed Paris and their friends. They longed for the life they had left behind.

In October, Hemingway was assigned to cover a story in New York City. He wanted to stay in Toronto, where his wife was about to give birth to their child, but the assistant editor insisted that he go. On October 10, 1923, as Hemingway was on his way back from this assignment, his son John Hadley Nicanor Hemingway was born. Hadley nicknamed him Bumby because he felt so warm and cuddly in her arms. Later, he was also called Jack.

By the time Bumby was three months old, his parents were on their way back to France. It was

January 1924, and another year of work, surprises, and life in Paris stretched out before the Hemingway family. They found an apartment at 113 rue Notre-Dame-des-champs. It was a great improvement over their old one. This building was on a tree-lined street with many cafés within walking distance. Some friends, the writer Ezra Pound and his wife, Dorothy, were close by, and it was a short walk to the lovely Luxembourg Gardens. However, this apartment was as noisy as their previous one because the owner operated a lumberyard and sawmill nearby.

Life continued at a normal pace for the Hemingways. It revolved around Hemingway's work and their son Bumby. Hemingway often wrote in a second bedroom that had been turned into an office. When it became too noisy at home, he escaped to a quiet café called the Closerie des Lilas. In his memoir, *A Moveable Feast*, Hemingway talked about working in this café:

> *Some days it went so well. . . . Then you would hear someone say, "Hi, Hem. What are you trying to do? Write in a café?"*
>
> *Your luck had run out and you shut the notebook. . . .*
>
> *I thought I would ignore him and see if I could write. . . .*
>
> *I went on and wrote another sentence. It dies hard when it is really going and you are into it.*[11]

In March 1924, *In Our Time* was published by a small firm called Three Mountains Press. Eventually, it was expanded into another book, also called *In Our Time*. The new edition was published by Boni and

Ernest, Hadley, and their infant son John ("Bumby") Hemingway on the slopes at Schruns, Austria.

Livewright, a New York publisher. Many of the stories in this book were set in Michigan and featured the character Nick Adams. When Hemingway sent copies of this book to his parents, they sent them back saying that the stories were filled with death and murder and were too violent. Book critics, on the other hand, liked *In Our Time* and wrote good reviews.

Hemingway was meeting more and more people and establishing a name for himself in the Paris literary community. It was inevitable that his social circle would grow to include people from all walks of life. Many of these people were wealthy, and they began to invite the Hemingways into their social circles.

In the summer of 1925, the Hemingways traveled to Pamplona, Spain, to follow the bullfights. They spent time with a group of people who later became the models for characters in Hemingway's first novel, *The Sun Also Rises*. It was also during this trip that Hemingway met Lady Duff Twysden, who inspired the main female character in *The Sun Also Rises*.

Hemingway, as well as some other men in the group, had focused their attention on Twysden, causing rivalry among the traveling companions. Hadley Hemingway, in her own quiet way, had also attracted an admirer. Her beauty inspired a handsome matador to give her his cape and a bull's ear.[12] These two events were enough to fire Hemingway's imagination and set in motion the plot for his first novel.

The story revolves around several characters who are in competition for the attention of the main female character, Brett Ashley. The first-person narrator, Jake Barnes, is an American newspaper reporter. The fictional matador Pedro Romero is based on real-life matador Cayetano Ordóñez. Robert Cohn, another character in the book, resembles another of Hemingway's friends in Spain, Harold Loeb.

The publication of this book caused hurt feelings among Hemingway's friends. Harold Loeb, in particular, thought Hemingway had shown him as a weak and vain person. Lady Duff Twysden decided to forgive Hemingway. If there were any doubts that Hemingway was combining fact with fiction in his writing, they were put to rest with the publication of his first novel. He had started the book in 1925, finished it in two months, and took another six months to revise it.

Included on this summer trip was another woman, Pauline Pfeiffer, whom the Hemingways had met through a mutual friend. At first, Hemingway did not pay much attention to the slender, attractive Pfeiffer. Yet, in the months to come, she would become a problem for both Ernest and Hadley Hemingway.

5

Fame, Fortune, and Loss

In 1926, while Hemingway was working on his first novel, he was also working on a second book, *The Torrents of Spring*, in which he criticized and satirized the work of novelists Sherwood Anderson and Gertrude Stein. These two writers had critiqued Hemingway's early work and helped to establish his writing contacts.

Was there a reason or excuse for Hemingway's bad behavior and disloyalty toward those people who considered him their friend? There is no doubt that Hemingway valued friendships. He once said that friends "stick together when things are impossible."[1] Still, one thing Hemingway's family, friends, and acquaintances soon found out was that they could, at any time, become a part of his literary work. He had no misgivings when it came to using people, places, and situations that he had known, visited, or experienced, in order to create his work. For him, fact and fiction were all a part of the creative process. He once told F. Scott Fitzgerald to "use in his writing the things that hurt him badly."[2]

Although Hemingway's writing life was going well, his personal world was changing. Pauline Pfeiffer, an American from a wealthy family, had become friends with Hadley and was often at their apartment, visiting or baby-sitting for Bumby. Eventually, Pfeiffer was included in their social lives. She was invited to dinners, on bike rides, and ski trips. In fact, she became part of their family. Gradually, Hemingway was drawn to Pfeiffer's glamorous appearance and intelligence, and they fell in love.

When Hadley Hemingway found out about their relationship, she asked them not to see each other for one hundred days. If at the end of this time they were still in love, she would grant Hemingway a divorce.[3] Pfeiffer temporarily moved to New York, and Hemingway's wife moved out of the apartment near the sawmill and into the Hotel Beauvoir. During this separation, Hemingway and his wife frequently saw each other. However, Hadley Hemingway did not wait for the one hundred days to end. She gave in when she saw how miserable her husband was.

In April 1927, Hemingway's first marriage ended after nearly six years. On May 10, 1927, he married Pauline Pfeiffer. After their marriage, Ernest and Pauline Hemingway continued to live in Paris, but in a more stylish fashion. They moved into an elegantly furnished apartment and traveled together throughout Europe.

Hemingway's next book was a collection of short stories called *Men Without Women*. These stories were rough-and-tumble ones, with lots of fighting and violence. The book sold well but once again was not popular with his parents because of the subject matter.

During the early part of 1928, Hemingway began a new novel, *A Farewell to Arms*. In April, the Hemingways decided to come back to the United States. They decided on Key West, Florida, delighted with this island full of coconut palms, guava trees, and lush flowers. They also liked the fact that there was very little traffic. During the early years, the island could be reached only by ferry from the American mainland or via Havana, Cuba. The influence of a Spanish/Cuban culture was evident in the language, foods, and architecture. One place, called Sloppy Joe's, was owned by Joe Russell, who became one of Hemingway's fishing companions. Sloppy Joe's was a favorite retreat for the writer because of the many different kinds of people who came into the saloon. Hemingway's imagination was put to good use at Sloppy Joe's.

A son, Patrick, was born on June 28, and Hemingway finished *A Farewell to Arms* in September of that year. Sadly, his father, ill with diabetes and heart disease, committed suicide by shooting himself on December 6 in Oak Park, Illinois. Hemingway told

Ernest Hemingway was drawn to Pauline Pfeiffer's glamour and intelligence, and in 1927 she became his second wife.

Max Perkins, his editor at Scribner's, how very deeply he had loved his father.[4]

Hemingway began rewriting *A Farewell to Arms* and wrote more than thirty versions before he was satisfied. The book was based on Hemingway's World War I experiences in Italy and his falling in love with the American nurse Agnes von Kurowsky. The main characters in the book are Lieutenant Frederic Henry, an American ambulance driver, and an English Red Cross nurse named Catherine Barkley. The story is narrated by Henry:

> *We had a lovely time that summer. When I could go out we rode in a carriage in the park. I remember the carriage, the horse going slowly, and up ahead the back of the driver with his varnished high hat, and Catherine Barkley sitting beside me.*[5]

All around them, battles are raging, and Lieutenant Henry can find no justification for war, as it claims its victims:

> *I was always embarrassed by the words sacred, glorious, and sacrifice and the expression in vain. . . . I had seen nothing sacred, and the things that were glorious had no glory. . . . Abstract words such as glory, honor, courage, or hallow were obscene beside the concrete names of villages, the numbers of regiments, and the dates.*[6]

A Farewell to Arms, Hemingway's second novel, was a popular and critical success. The book is still considered one of the great stories of love and war and a masterpiece of fiction.

After a vacation in Paris, the Hemingways bought a house in Key West in the spring of 1931, when Pauline was pregnant with their son Gregory. Pauline's Uncle Gus paid for the two-story Spanish Colonial–style white stone house built around 1851. The house needed lots of repairs, but the property included lush gardens and a carriage house in the back. Pauline Hemingway later installed a saltwater swimming pool. The Hemingways lived in Key West for twelve years. Hemingway's first son, Bumby, often visited there and played with his half-brothers Patrick and Gregory ("Gigi").

Hemingway quickly settled into a pleasant routine of writing in the mornings and then fishing or socializing in the afternoons and evenings. His writing habits were well established by this time. He would rise early, work until twelve or one o'clock, and then stop, knowing where he would begin writing the next day. He also made it a rule never to write on Sunday because he considered it unlucky. He read during his off hours so he would not think about writing until the next day. In the afternoons, after lunch, he often went deep-sea fishing. He also enjoyed visiting with friends, taking walks, and stopping at favorite spots for a drink.

As much as Hemingway enjoyed life in Key West, it was not in his nature to stay in one place for long periods. In the summers, when Key West became too hot for the Hemingways, the now famous author headed north to cooler places. One destination was the beautiful woods and mountains of Wyoming and Montana. The Hemingway family stayed in a cabin at

Ernest and Pauline check on the day's catch with their sons Patrick, Gregory, and Bumby.

the L-Bar-T Ranch, with a view of Yellowstone National Park. It was here that Hemingway indulged his love of the outdoors and nature, fishing for trout, and hunting big game such as elk and grizzly bear. Ernest Hemingway was not a man to stand still, not when there was so much in life to do and see.

6

A Life of Adventure

It did not matter whether Hemingway was hunting for bear in Montana, following the bullfights in Spain, or covering a war as a foreign correspondent, it was almost always certain that he was working on an article, short story, or book. He once told a friend how he had written *A Farewell to Arms*: The manuscript had been carried around and worked on in Paris, Key West, Arkansas, Kansas City, and Wyoming.[1]

His next book after *A Farewell to Arms* was a nonfiction one, *Death in the Afternoon*, about Spanish bullfighting. In this book, Hemingway explained the techniques used in bullfighting and portrayed the culture and history of the Spanish people. He wanted to show that there was beauty and nobility in the "Corrida de Toros" (bullfights). Hemingway considered bullfighting an art form in which certain skills, emotions, and bravery were necessary in order to do a good job. He admired the famous matadors of the time such as Manolo Bienvenida, Domingo Ortega, and Marcial Lalanda.

Hemingway had been fascinated with the Spanish bullfight from the first time he had seen one. He was drawn to the bravery of the matador and the bull, the danger of the sport, and the idea of displaying grace under pressure. He became a true aficionado of bullfighting, meeting with and becoming friends with the best matadors of the day. He even went so far as to participate in a roundup of young bulls gathered in a bullring, where people were allowed to run with the bulls to test their own bravery. The horns of the yearlings were padded to prevent serious injury, but it was still a frightening experience to get into a bullring with charging, snorting young bulls.

Death in the Afternoon was published by Charles Scribner's Sons in October 1932. The reviews were mixed. One of the harshest was from a critic named Max Eastman, who titled his book review "Bull in the Afternoon," suggesting that Hemingway was not as brave as he pretended to be. Hemingway was not too happy with this unfair description of his labor of love and showed it when he happened to see Eastman at the publisher's office. He hit Eastman with a book.[2] The two men scuffled, but no one got hurt.

Hemingway's book on Africa, *Green Hills of Africa*, also came out of his love for adventure. In November

1933, Pauline and Ernest Hemingway sailed aboard the SS *General Metzinger* for an African safari that lasted for nearly three months. This trip was paid for by Pfeiffer's Uncle Gus. Hemingway's friend Charles Thompson and a hunter named Philip Percival were also included in the trip. This African adventure contributed to Hemingway's persona as a man who could do almost anything. Added to his growing list of accomplishments was big-game hunter.

The safari was a successful one, even though Hemingway came down with amoebic dysentery (a parasitic disease) and had to be flown out to Nairobi for treatment. When he was better, he flew back to the safari site and returned to hunting lion, cheetah, gazelle, antelope, leopard, and buffalo. Africa, with its wild beauty, majestic mountains, and abundant wildlife, left a lasting impression on Hemingway, both as a man and as a writer. He had tested his manhood by hunting animals that could easily have killed him. In addition, he also acquired a love for the land and the people.

When they returned to Key West in the spring of 1934, Hemingway wrote *Green Hills of Africa*, published in 1935. He also wrote two of his best short stories, "The Snows of Kilimanjaro" and "The Short Happy Life of Francis Macomber." Both stories deal with male/female relationships, bravery, and death, and both were later made into movies.

It wasn't long before Hemingway was eager to start on yet another adventure. This time, it was deep-sea fishing in the warm waters of the Caribbean. Hemingway ordered a thirty-eight-foot, diesel-powered boat with two engines, double rudders, and a speed of sixteen knots at full power. The boat could sleep up to eight people. He paid $75,000 for it and named it the *Pilar*, after the patron saint of Zaragoza, a Spanish town that he loved.

Hemingway spent many happy hours on the *Pilar*, writing, fishing for marlin, and enjoying time with his sons and friends. As with his African adventure, Hemingway once again showed his capacity for enjoying a sport and proving he was good at it. Using his own methods of deep-sea fishing, Hemingway often returned home with a gigantic marlin or tuna weighing more than three hundred pounds. He was tireless when he was fighting a fish, sometimes staying with it for hours at a time. Eventually, the fish grew tired. Occasionally Hemingway gave up—but this was something that almost never happened.

During these many adventures, Hemingway's second wife, Pauline, tried to spend as much time as possible with her husband. She hired nannies for their two sons so she would have time to accompany Hemingway on hunting and fishing trips. In addition, Pauline had become an important critic of his work. As a family, the Hemingways shared many good times with Bumby, Patrick, and Gigi. The second Mrs. Hemingway treated Bumby as her own son.

Unfortunately, Pauline Hemingway could not prevent her husband from being attracted to other women. Soon another woman came into Hemingway's life. She was an attractive blonde and a published writer. This time Hemingway was older than his

Hemingway's beloved boat, the Pilar, *in Key West, Florida.*

new love interest. He was thirty-seven, and Martha Gellhorn was twenty-eight.

Gellhorn and Hemingway met at Sloppy Joe's in Key West, where Hemingway usually spent time after his morning writing sessions. It was December 1936 and Gellhorn was on vacation with her mother and brother. They had decided to take a bus from Miami to Key West for a day's outing. The two writers found they had similar interests. She liked to travel and had an adventurous spirit. She was feisty and daring, qualities Hemingway liked in women. But Gellhorn was also fiercely independent and competitive and intent on earning her own way. She had already published a novel in 1934 called *What Mad Pursuit* and a collection of short stories in 1936 called *The Trouble I've Seen*. It was clear she would not put up with any disrespect or second-class-citizen status from the strong-willed Hemingway.

In January 1937, Hemingway and Gellhorn went their separate ways but kept in touch through letters. Hemingway was working on a new project, *To Have and Have Not*, his only novel set in the United States. In this book, Hemingway tackled the theme of the struggling working class versus the rich in the years following the Great Depression. His main character, Harry Morgan, is the owner of a cabin cruiser. Morgan is out of work and is trying to survive by illegally transporting bootleggers between Cuba and the United States.

Hemingway's schedule, as usual, was a hectic one. In February 1937, he left for Spain to cover the Spanish Civil War as a foreign correspondent for

NANA, the North American Newspaper Alliance. A month later, Gellhorn traveled to Spain as well, hoping to cover the war for *Collier's* magazine.

Hemingway found his match in the fearless and ambitious Gellhorn. It was clear from the beginning that this was to be different from his other relationships. Unlike the other women in his life, who had given up their own needs to be totally dedicated to Hemingway, Gellhorn was not about to do the same. She was just as persistent as Hemingway in pursuing a writing career. She would go to any length to get a story, even if that meant getting the top news story before Hemingway did.

Most important, Gellhorn was not going to cater to Hemingway's every whim or desire, or be overpowered by his strong, controlling personality. Their tastes in friends and social activities were different. Hemingway at times socialized with people who were rough and noisy, while Gellhorn was more proper and tidy. Still, they were drawn to each other. He was attracted to her sharp wit and fearless personality, and she to his talent. Gellhorn could not resist his strong pursuit of her.

For a while, they were good for each other. Gellhorn was learning things about the newspaper business and reporting through his experienced eyes. He encouraged her to write about the Spanish Civil War, and eventually she became the foreign correspondent for *Collier's*. This position enabled her to travel to the war fronts, where she visited the wounded and saw firsthand what war was really like.

Occasionally, Hemingway and Gellhorn traveled

together to the war fronts, where there was always the risk of getting caught in enemy fire. Gellhorn showed courage in these dangerous situations, which was a trait that Hemingway admired in both men and women. He was no stranger to his own brand of bravery during the Spanish Civil War. The war had begun in 1936 when General Francisco Franco led his fascist forces in a rebellion against the Republican central government (the Loyalists). Hemingway found himself siding with the Republic.

Hemingway placed himself in many dangerous situations in order to report on the war for NANA. He stayed in the Hotel Florida in Madrid, which was regularly bombed, and he was often out in the field covering the war. Somehow, during this difficult period, he wrote a play called *The Fifth Column* and worked on a Spanish documentary by the Dutch director Joris Ivens. This film, *The Spanish Earth*, supported the Loyalist cause. Its Hollywood debut raised thousands of dollars for ambulances and other equipment needed in Spain.

During this period of traveling to and from the United States, Hemingway was also seeing Gellhorn whenever they could coordinate their schedules. Hemingway's wife, Pauline, knew there were difficulties in their marriage. Yet she hoped her husband would come to his senses and return to the marriage they had shared for the past ten years. They met several times during this period, but it was clear that the writer was more concerned with writing about the Spanish Civil War than with saving his marriage.[3]

Hemingway covered the war from 1937 to 1938

until it became clear that the Loyalists were losing to Franco's forces. NANA then canceled Hemingway's contract, so he returned to the United States and his home in Key West. By this time, both Hemingway and his wife knew their marriage was over. His interest in Martha Gellhorn and the pain he had seen in war-torn Spain stood between him and Pauline. They no longer shared the same interests or concerns but were unsure of how to deal with the complicated situation. Hemingway threw himself into a new book, while his wife tried to keep their marriage together. But it was obvious that their marriage was on hold until they resolved their differences.

For two years, the Hemingways struggled on in their crumbling marriage, although they were separated most of the time. In the meantime, Martha Gellhorn continued traveling around the world as a correspondent for *Collier's*, still meeting with Hemingway whenever she could. Then, in October 1940, Hemingway's fifth novel was published.

For Whom the Bell Tolls is set during the Spanish Civil War. The hero, Robert Jordan, is an American professor of Spanish who has come to Spain to fight on the side of the Loyalists. He falls in love with a Spanish girl named Maria. The tragic love story is told against the background of a war-torn country and the struggle for survival. Hemingway took his title for the book from a seventeenth-century meditation by John Donne on the human condition. It begins:

"No man is an Iland; intire of it selfe; every man is a peece of the Continent, a part of the maine." Then it finishes, "any man's death diminishes me, because I am involved in Mankinde; and therefore, never send to know for whom the bell tolls; It tolls for thee."[4]

Immensely popular, *For Whom the Bell Tolls* became the biggest seller in American fiction since Margaret Mitchell's *Gone with the Wind* in 1936. One reviewer called it Hemingway's best book, predicting that it would become one of American literature's major novels. It also became a hit movie featuring Ingrid Bergman and Gary Cooper, two top movie stars of the time.

7

Papa

Through the years, Hemingway had acquired another nickname in addition to those early ones of Hemingstein, Ernie, Nesto, and Stein. As early as his thirties, he was already being called "Papa," an affectionate term used by his wives, sons, and friends. In time, this respectful title became a part of his image, his legend. Papa, now in his early forties, was living in Cuba in a country farmhouse called Finca Vigia, which means Lookout Farm.

The story of how Hemingway finally came to spend nearly twenty years of his life in Cuba is an interesting one. Hemingway had traveled to Havana, Cuba, during his separation from his second wife. He rented a small room in the Ambos Mundos Hotel. Gellhorn thought the place was depressing and felt Hemingway needed a better place to live and work while his divorce was being finalized. Gellhorn found Finca Vigia in the classified ads section of a Havana newspaper. She immediately took Hemingway to see the farmhouse, which was located several miles outside Havana on a hill near the town of San Francisco de Paula. It was situated on a high point above the sea with a view of the Gulf Stream and the sparkling night lights of Havana. At first, Hemingway decided against renting the house because it was so run-down and, he thought, too far from Havana. Gellhorn, however, was not discouraged. While he was away on a fishing trip, she had repairs made to the house and brought Hemingway back to see it. This time, he agreed to rent the house for one year.

Hemingway soon fell in love with Finca Vigia, which dated back to the early 1900s. It was surrounded by lush flowers, palm and almond trees, and eighteen varieties of mango trees. In the front of the house was an old ceiba tree, considered the sacred tree of Cuba. Its roots were so long and strong that they extended under the house, making some of the floors uneven and lifting floor tiles in certain places. The ceiba tree was estimated to be nearly one hundred years old, and possibly as old as one hundred fifty years. The house also had a swimming pool and tennis courts. Best of all, Finca Vigia was located not far from the Gulf Stream. Hemingway kept his boat, the *Pilar*, docked in the village of Cojimar. He and his boat captain, Gregorio Fuentes, would often disappear on the *Pilar* for long deep-sea fishing trips.

Hemingway lived in his home in Cuba, called Finca Vigia, for nearly twenty years.

Fuentes and Hemingway became good friends. Years later, after Hemingway died, Fuentes said that Hemingway had a good heart and that he loved Hemingway like a brother.[1]

In November 1940, Hemingway divorced his second wife. A few weeks later he married Martha Gellhorn. A month after that, he bought Finca Vigia from its owner, a Frenchman named Joseph D'Orn Duchamp. Hemingway paid $18,500 for his new home, which became his permanent long-term residence. He became known as San Francisco de Paula's famous celebrity, the writer who lived high on the hill.

Although Hemingway was busy with his own life and writing, he still found the time to be involved with the people living near him and in the town of San Francisco de Paula. One story goes that Hemingway bought baseball gloves, balls, bats, and uniforms for a group of children after he had discovered them throwing stones at his mango trees to knock down the fruit. He didn't mind their taking the fruit, but he did not like their hitting the trees. When someone told him the boys were only practicing to be baseball players, he decided they should be playing baseball instead of throwing stones at his fruit trees. The baseball team that developed from this incident became known as "Las Estrellas de Gigi" (Gigi's Stars), named after his third son, Gregory.[2]

Throughout the years that Hemingway lived in Cuba, he shared his home with more than fifty cats. They had their own sleeping and eating area on the first floor of a three-story addition to the house. Some of the cats' names were Boise, Crazy Christian,

Missouri, Ambrosy, and Spendy. Boise was Hemingway's favorite cat. It was given to him by Fuentes, his boat captain. He also had a favorite dog, Black Dog, who was a faithful companion. Black Dog often stayed near Hemingway when he was writing.

At this stage of his life, Hemingway was set in his ways. He wrote in the mornings, usually standing up at a makeshift worktable that was the top of a bookcase near his bed. There was a large desk in the room, but its surface was cluttered with stacks of papers, books, newspaper clippings, and a variety of other items. He preferred to stand and type at his worktable while he read the handwritten pages from a wooden reading-board. At the end of a writing day, he noted his daily output of words on a large chart. The rest of the day would be spent fishing, reading, and socializing in the evenings. If he had not written the amount he had hoped for that day, he would make up for it the next day.[3]

After marrying Gellhorn, he was more content to stay at home instead of globe-trotting. He still needed to seek out new challenges and adventures, but less frequently. Hemingway wanted his new wife to stay at home, take care of the house, and spend time with him. Gellhorn had other ideas. She was nine years younger than her husband and anxious to continue traveling around the world. She was a reporter and wanted to cover important news events. She was not much of a housekeeper and preferred to leave the running of the house and the cooking to others. She did enjoy spending time with Hemingway's sons when they visited during summer vacations and holidays,

In 1940, Hemingway married writer Martha Gellhorn. Shown here are Ernest and Martha Hemingway at Finca Vigia with his son Gregory and her mother.

but she did not always like the group of friends that her husband invited to their home. She thought them too loud, rough, and messy.

By January 1941, Hemingway and Gellhorn were off to report on China's struggle against Japan. Hemingway believed that China would fall to the Communists and that the United States would go to war with Japan.[4] He had signed a contract with *PM*, a New York newspaper, and Gellhorn had an agreement to report for *Collier's* magazine. The trip to China was tiresome and difficult, but Hemingway held up well during the long trip over the Burma Road to Rangoon and back.

Even so, the China trip fatigued him, and he was anxious to get back home. The trip also tired Gellhorn, but she was still energized enough to continue her assignments for *Collier's*. She wanted to go to Europe again to cover World War II, but this time she could not persuade her husband to go with her. Instead, he stayed in Cuba and involved himself in a project closer to home. Gellhorn had no interest in his new adventure, so she disappeared on yet another assignment, leaving Hemingway to put his new plan into action.

Hemingway's new plan was a dangerous adventure in which he and some friends, whom he called the "Crook Factory," would patrol Cuban waters looking for German U-boats. He gained permission from the Cuban government, and in May 1942 the "Crook Factory" became a new participant in the war. For one year, the *Pilar* served as a spy boat, staying at sea for days at a time, and once for nearly two months. Its main purpose was to locate German U-boat activity in the Caribbean and then report the whereabouts to the proper authorities. Although the *Pilar* never came in direct contact with a German vessel, Hemingway and his crew managed to report German activity, thus helping the Navy to sink some German submarines.

Hemingway was finally persuaded by his wife to give up his spying activities and to return to the safety of Finca Vigia. But instead of staying there with him, she was planning yet another trip. She wanted them to travel together to Europe as war correspondents.

Hemingway, competitive by nature, agreed to go, but he did something that would seriously hurt his relationship with Gellhorn. He offered his services as a foreign correspondent to *Collier's* magazine, causing Gellhorn to lose her job. Wartime rules allowed a magazine only one frontline correspondent. *Collier's* jumped at the chance to have the famous author write stories for the magazine, so the editors gave the job to Hemingway and fired Gellhorn.

It was understandable that Gellhorn was furious with her husband for throwing his weight around as a big-name writer. Whatever the reason for his behavior, Hemingway showed up in Europe alone to begin his reporting.

Soon after his arrival, Hemingway was in a car crash that gave him a nasty scalp cut and a concussion. Gellhorn reunited with her husband when she visited him in a London hospital after his accident. It was a distant and cold meeting, because Gellhorn was angry with Hemingway for taking her job, and she told him so.[5] Hemingway was looking for sympathy, but

Gellhorn was not the type of woman to offer kind words when she felt she had been treated unfairly. She just ignored him.

Papa soon found comfort with another woman. Also a foreign correspondent, Mary Welsh would learn to cater to the famous writer's large ego and many demands.

Hemingway, true to his nature of getting to the action of a story, became intensely involved in reporting on World War II. *Collier's* planned to feature Hemingway's account of the 1944 D-day invasion and to include a short report from Martha Gellhorn. Although he was still suffering from the effects of his concussion, Hemingway managed to view the D-day landing on Omaha Beach from an attack transport. Gellhorn, in her own style, went one step further by actually going ashore with the troops after she had hidden away on a hospital ship! She helped bring wounded men back to the ship. Hemingway was so annoyed that his wife had gotten closer to the action than he had that he denied she had ever done such a thing.[6]

Unfortunately, Hemingway's insistence on being closer to the action caused him more physical problems. He hurt his head as he dived into a ditch to avoid German anti-tank gunfire. This injury caused severe headaches, ringing ears, and dizziness. In addition to his physical injuries, he was upset when he learned that his eldest son, John (Bumby), an officer in the Office of Strategic Services, had been captured by the Germans after parachuting into France in October 1944. As if he didn't have enough troubles,

Hemingway also came down with pneumonia. On top of that, when he was finally reunited with his wife, they had a big argument. Hemingway's marriage of five years to the strong-willed Martha Gellhorn was unofficially over.

In March 1945, Hemingway flew back to the United States. In April, his son John was released from a prisoner-of-war camp. Mary Welsh, his new love, joined Hemingway and his sons in Cuba. He was eager to begin another serious piece of writing and started to work on a new book, *Islands in the Stream.* Things were definitely looking up for the troubled writer.

In December 1945, Hemingway's third divorce became final. On March 14, 1946, Hemingway married his fourth wife, Mary Welsh. His nicknames for her were Pickle, Kittner, and Miss Mary. At the time of her marriage, Welsh was thirty-eight and Hemingway, forty-seven. She had been married twice before, once in her early twenties and again when she was thirty. Welsh was the only child of Adeline and Tom Welsh and had been close to her father, who was a logger and operator of a Mississippi riverboat. She had spent many lazy, summer days with her father on the riverboat and enjoyed the adventure and freedom that this type of life offered.

Welsh shared many of Hemingway's interests. She enjoyed fishing, skiing, hunting, and traveling, and she liked to entertain. She was also a good cook and organizer and kept Finca Vigia running smoothly. Under Welsh's guidance, their Cuban home blossomed into a comfortable and orderly residence. She had the pool repaired, added a guest house, and had a tower built onto the house for Papa's study and as a place to house his many cats. She also planted a rose and vegetable garden. Most important, Mary Welsh was willing to give up her freedom and independence in order to become the kind of wife that Ernest Hemingway wanted. In addition, she became very protective of Papa. Still, they had their difficulties, especially when she could not tolerate some of his behavior. It was then that they would have bitter arguments. In spite of their differences, though, Hemingway always claimed to "truly love Miss Mary."[7]

In 1950, Ernest Hemingway was fifty-one years old. His health had deteriorated badly from too much alcohol and overeating. He had high blood pressure, and his drinking was affecting his liver. In addition to working on *Islands in the Stream*, he began another book, *Garden of Eden*. Both books would remain unpublished during his lifetime. Hemingway liked to write books and put them "in the bank," a term he used when his books were put away and allowed to ripen until they were ready to be published.[8]

He did have a book published in 1950. *Across the River and into the Trees* is set in Venice, Italy, one of Hemingway's favorite places. It is the story of a young woman, Renata, and an older man. The character of Renata is supposedly based on a dark-haired Venetian girl named Adriana Ivancich. Hemingway had met her in 1948 while visiting friends in Italy. Soon, he was calling her "daughter," a term of endearment he used for women he had grown to like or even love. Hemingway's romantic nature and his vivid imagination took over as he created a love story between his characters: the eighteen-year-old Contessa Renata and a fifty-year-old American colonel, Richard Cantwell. As portrayed in the book, it was a love that could never become a reality. In real life, his own romantic feelings for the equally young Adriana Ivancich could not come true.

The themes in *Across the River and into the Trees* deal with youth, growing old, and looking back on one's life. Hemingway spent nearly two years working on this book. It was the new novel everyone was waiting for, but it was attacked by critics. One reviewer called it the author's worst novel.[9] Hemingway was disappointed, but he continued with his work, refusing to believe his best writing was behind him.

Unfortunately, life did not improve for the aging author. In 1951, his mother died, and then his second wife, Pauline, unexpectedly passed away. Not long after these losses, Hemingway's longtime editor at Charles Scribner's Sons, Max Perkins, died. If Hemingway had been avoiding facing his own mortality, it was now staring him straight in the face. Still, the famous writer was not physically or mentally finished. He would challenge his body one more time on another big adventure. In addition, he would also write his best book, a small classic that would redeem his status as one of the most influential writers of the twentieth century.

8

More Adventures

It is an interesting fact that Hemingway's Pulitzer Prize–winning novel, *The Old Man and the Sea*, did not start out as a separate book. It was intended to be part of a larger work about the earth, sea, and air. Instead, Hemingway decided to concentrate on the sea section, which became a 120-page novella of 2,700 words, first published in *Life* magazine.

Hemingway and his wife Mary were out on his boat, the *Pilar*, when the Pulitzer Prize award was announced in 1953. Hemingway was so excited by the acceptance of his new work that he quickly planned another trip to Europe and an African safari. His son Patrick was a big-game hunter living in

Tanganyika (now the republic of Tanzania). It was a good opportunity for Hemingway to see his son and to go on a second safari. Mary Hemingway planned to accompany her husband, taking her first African trip.

Hemingway contacted Philip Percival, the guide on his previous safari, and made the arrangements. However, before Hemingway could get away, he had to finalize a movie deal to film *The Old Man and the Sea*, starring the famous actor Spencer Tracy. There were also other business and family commitments and last-minute details and preparations to attend to before he could leave. Finally, by May 1953, the Hemingways were on their way to New York and their sea voyage to France, where they would visit old friends. Then it was on to Spain to see the bullfights at Pamplona and to celebrate Hemingway's fifty-fourth birthday in Madrid.

The Hemingways traveled between Spain and France until late July. Then they stayed in France and waited until it was time to board the ship for their trip to Mombassa, Kenya, to begin their African safari. They had planned to be away for many months, so naturally they had packed many items to take with them. They had more than fifty pieces of luggage, bags of books to read, guns, cameras, and, of course, Hemingway's typewriter. Finally, by August 6, Ernest and Mary Hemingway were on a ship heading for their African destination. Two weeks later, the Hemingways arrived in Mombassa. Philip Percival, their safari guide, was there on the docks to greet them. He drove them to their campsite near Percival's farm, Kitanga.

Percival was a well-known hunter who had guided and hunted with Teddy Roosevelt and the Duke of Windsor. He had retired from big-game hunting, but Hemingway had persuaded the pleasant and skilled Percival to take on yet another safari.

From this first of two camps, they traveled to the second one, where the safari camp workers had already set up their tents. Percival had obtained permission from the Kenya Game Department to hunt within the African National Game Reserve. The safari was not only about hunting. It was also about listening to native stories and legends around the campfire and learning about African culture and languages.

There were occasional breaks from the safari. The Hemingways visited Patrick Hemingway, who had become ill with malaria. They stayed until he was feeling better. On another occasion they also headed back to Percival's farm for a short visit.

From August 1953 to early January 1954, the safari went well. The hunting was good, and there were no major disruptions or problems. However, in mid-January, two events happened that upset Hemingway's well-being for the rest of his life.

Hemingway had decided, with all good intentions, to give his wife a belated Christmas present. He rented a Cessna 180 and hired a bush pilot named Roy Marsh to fly them over some scenic African sights. They would see Lake Albert and the spectacular Murchison Falls where the Nile River falls through a rock cleft and descends into cascading pools of water

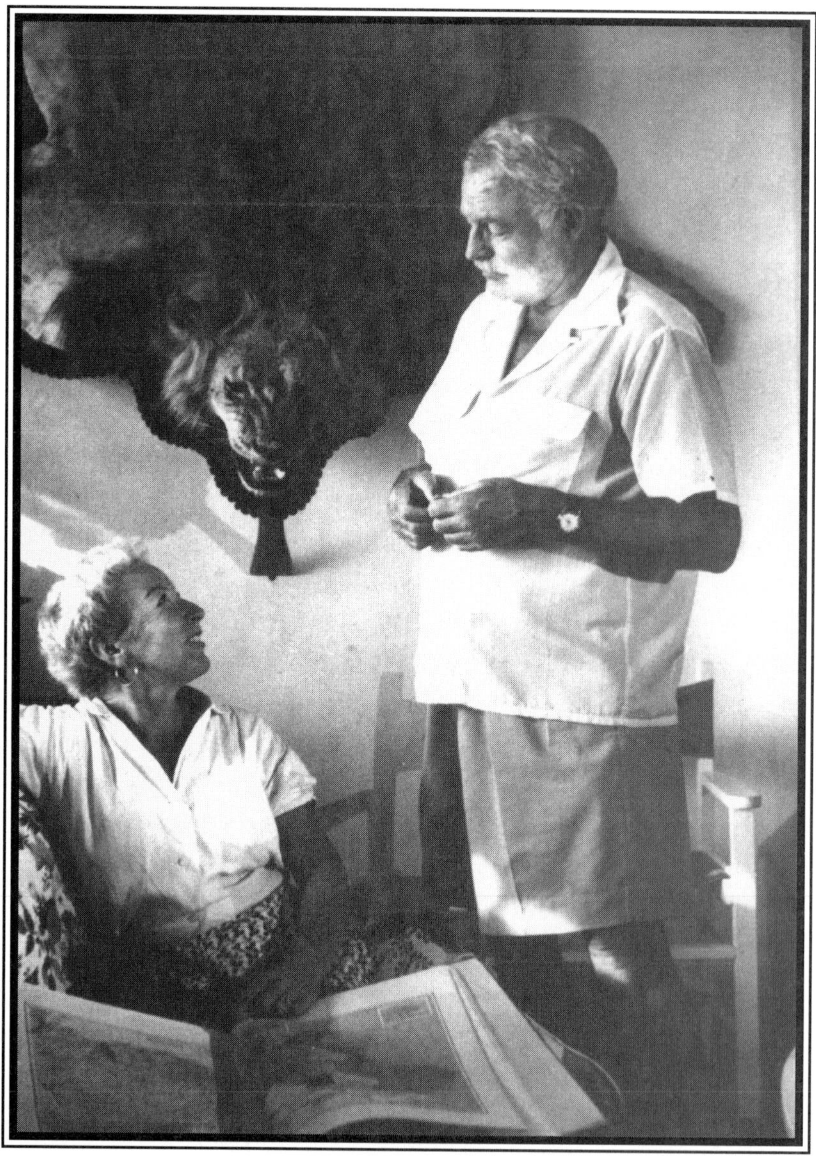

Mary Welsh shared Hemingway's interest in travel and adventure. This photograph of the couple was taken in the mid-1950s.

several hundred feet below. Mary Hemingway shot roll after roll of film as the bush pilot circled the falls several times. Suddenly, a flight of ibis, birds with long legs and long curved bills, flew in front of the plane. Marsh dove quickly to avoid hitting them. Unfortunately, the plane hit an abandoned telegraph wire that stretched across the gorge, causing the plane to crash. They were all stranded on rocky ground in a secluded area of thorn trees in Uganda. Luckily, no one was seriously injured, although Hemingway's wife had cracked some ribs and was in shock. After making camp on a high point of land, away from the river, they wondered how they would get help. The plane's radio wasn't working. They spent a sleepless night on the hill listening to the night sounds and worrying about danger from the elephants gathered nearby.

The next morning, a large white boat appeared on the river, but the skipper was not eager to take them aboard. Finally, the matter was settled when Hemingway offered to pay the skipper a large sum of money.

When the rescue boat reached its home port at Butiaba, Hemingway and his wife were rushed onto a plane to fly to Entebbe. News reporters were waiting there to find out what tragedy had befallen the famous writer and his wife. It seemed that someone had spotted their downed plane and reported that there were no survivors. News had gone out that the Hemingways had been killed in a plane crash! The couple needed prompt medical attention and were exhausted from their overnight experience, but first the reporters wanted to get the story on the celebrity writer and his wife.

Ironically, the plane the Hemingways were rushed onto had difficulty getting off the ground. Mary Hemingway later described this frightening event: "We lifted slightly, set down, lifted again like a grasshopper, set down again, continued hopping, the tail bumping. . . . Then came the wrenching, creaking, crashing, breaking and we were stopped and flames were leaping outside my window."[1]

Everyone managed to escape again. This time, though, Hemingway suffered a serious injury to his head when he used it to butt open a jammed door. His scalp was cut and he had another concussion along with first-degree burns. He received emergency treatment, but it wasn't until a few months later that more serious injuries were finally diagnosed. Hemingway had suffered damage to his liver, spleen, and kidney, hearing loss, temporary vision loss in one eye, and a crushed vertebra.

The Hemingways stayed in Africa, but the injured writer was not well. During this time, he lost twenty pounds from his large burly frame. He appeared smaller and frail, his shoulders were slouched, and his hair was white. He was depressed and suffering from terrible back pain. The two plane crashes that had occurred within two days of each other had taken their toll on him. Still, he did not return home but continued with the safari until he experienced yet another injury. While trying to put out a brushfire near camp, he fell into the flames. He suffered second-degree burns on his legs, chest, abdomen, lips, left hand, and right forearm. This accident brought the safari to an end. Living life to the fullest was finally catching up with the American legend.

The Hemingways still did not return to their Cuban home. In late March 1954, they traveled to Venice, Italy, where Hemingway managed to write, visit friends, and do some reading. He spent a lot of time in bed because of his poor health and was in a terrible mood most of the time. Yet Hemingway was not willing to give in to his injuries. In April he was traveling again. This time he went to Spain, alone. Mary Hemingway needed a break from her husband, so she took a trip to Paris and London and later joined Hemingway in Spain.

Finally, in June 1954, the Hemingways returned to Finca Vigia, after being away for more than a year. On July 21, Hemingway celebrated his fifty-fifth birthday. He was still recovering from his injuries, and his health would never be the same again. His blood pressure was high, his liver was not functioning properly, and he suffered from kidney infections. In addition, he had been drinking heavily to dull the constant back pain caused by the injuries he had suffered in the plane crashes. A life of hard living and the physical injuries were taking their toll, yet Hemingway was still moving on with his life and work.

Good news arrived for Hemingway in the fall of 1954. On the morning of October 28, 1954, he awoke early to begin his daily routine of writing from about 6:00 A.M. to noon. But this morning, his routine was interrupted by a phone call informing him that he had just won the prestigious Nobel Prize for Literature. The Nobel Prize was named after a Swedish chemist, Alfred B. Nobel, who had made his fortune by inventing dynamite. It was established to give recognition for impressive achievements in areas such as science, medicine, literature, and peace.

After Hemingway hung up the phone, he went to awaken Mary to share the good news. Although it was an exciting time for both of them, the news that Hemingway had won the award did not come as a complete surprise. There had been rumors circulating among the media that Hemingway was going to be the new Nobel Prize winner in literature.

If anyone deserved the Nobel Prize, it was Ernest Miller Hemingway, who, by the age of fifty-five, had written close to twenty books, many short stories, newspaper and magazine articles, poetry, and a play. The Nobel Prize selection committee had noted that Hemingway's contribution to literature was the "powerful, style-making mastery of the art of modern narration."[2]

Hemingway was both amused and humbled by the attention the award generated. He once said he thought Carl Sandburg, who wrote a six-volume biography of Abraham Lincoln, was as much or more deserving than he of the Nobel Prize, as was Isak Dinesen, who wrote *Out of Africa.*[3]

As soon as the award was announced, hordes of people descended upon his home in Cuba. Reporters wanted his reactions to winning the award. Photographers wanted to take pictures of the author in his home, at work, or even when relaxing. The

The first edition of The Old Man and the Sea *was published in 1952 with this illustration on the cover. A year later, the book won the Pulitzer Prize in Literature.*

telephone rang constantly with magazine editors and writers requesting interviews. Uninvited people dropped by his home at all times of the day just to meet or speak with him. Old friends showed up at his doorstep. Letters of congratulations poured in, many of which were answered by Mary Hemingway. In the beginning, Hemingway granted many interviews, spending hours with writers and photographers, but eventually he began to turn down the requests. The constant distractions were interrupting his work schedule.

Hemingway, nevertheless, did try to meet the demands placed upon him. He was meeting with people, continuing to write, and trying to recover from his injuries from the two plane crashes. But unfortunately, there was one thing he could not do. He could not attend the Nobel Prize award ceremonies in Stockholm to accept the $35,000 check and gold medal. He announced that he was too ill to travel. Also, although he did not say this, he did not like to give speeches. Instead, he wrote a gracious acceptance speech, which John Cabot, the U.S. ambassador to Stockholm, read at the award ceremonies. Toward the end of the speech, Hemingway wrote, "It is because we have had such great writers in the past that a writer is driven far out past where he can go, out to where no one can help him. I have spoken too long for a writer. A writer should write what he has to say and not speak it. Again I thank you."[4]

The months after the award ceremonies were hectic ones. Hemingway was pleased with the award, but the attention that came with it was a mixed blessing.

There were the constant invasions of his privacy when reporters, friends, strangers, photographers, and others popped up at Finca Vigia at all hours of the day. The isolation and level of concentration that he needed for his work were continually interrupted. He had been working on a book about Africa, but after writing several thousand words he wrapped it in cellophane and put it aside because he could no longer concentrate on it. Instead, he turned his attention to writing some short stories.

It was evident to Hemingway's family and friends that this strong, vibrant, and fun-loving man was aging quickly. His once powerful shoulders were now stooped. The long legs that moved his six-foot frame were now weak and shaky. His hair was white and thinning, and he had grown a beard, also white, to cover skin irritations. His clear, sharp mind was having difficulty turning his thoughts into written words. Hemingway was determined to improve his health and to continue his writing, but life was changing for him. Advancing age, physical injury, and the inability to write with intensity created a constant challenge for him. During the remaining years of his life, the challenges of writing, like mountain climbing, to reach higher and more difficult peaks were growing steeper and steeper and farther out of reach.

9

No More Mountains to Climb

By August 1956, Hemingway's health had improved enough for him to take another trip to Europe. Although he still had recurring health problems, he and his wife sailed on the *Ile de France* and arrived in France in September. They planned to stay in Paris, then travel to Spain to watch the bullfights. From there, they would move on to Africa for a safari with Hemingway's son Patrick.

The Hemingways' travel itinerary was an ambitious one, especially in light of their illnesses. While on vacation, Mary Hemingway suffered from colitis and Hemingway had a much-needed physical examination. The medical tests showed that his blood pressure and cholesterol count were too high and his liver was inflamed. The doctor put him on a strict nonfat diet and recommended he reduce his alcohol consumption. In addition, he suggested that Hemingway cancel his African plans. Hemingway responded that he could last for one more trip.[1] Eventually, though, he did cancel the safari trip, in part because of the closing of the Suez Canal and his medical problems.

Toward the end of November 1956, the Hemingways returned to the Ritz Hotel in Paris, where the author was in for a pleasant surprise. The story goes that an older porter carrying Hemingway's luggage told him of two small trunks that were sitting in the hotel basement. They had been left there by Hemingway more than twenty-five years earlier, and he had forgotten about them. When Hemingway opened the trunks, he said, he was overjoyed to find his old blue notebooks, typed fiction, and newspaper clippings of his early Paris years.[2]

The discovery could not have come at a better time, mainly because he was having so much difficulty with his writing. The notebooks brought back pleasant memories, although some scholars today question the exact contents of the trunks. In any case, the forgotten items helped him recall and recreate the past for a memoir titled *A Moveable Feast*. It was a collection of sketches about his youthful marriage to Hadley Richardson, his friendships with Gertrude Stein and F. Scott Fitzgerald, his early writing days in Paris, and other memories. He worked on this book for a few years and didn't finish it until 1960. It was not published until after his death.

By the winter of 1957, Hemingway was back in Cuba. He was not doing well mentally or physically. In general, he was depressed and frustrated at the way his body had become old and weak. Still, he was planning to work on *A Moveable Feast* and an article on bullfighting that he had agreed to write for *Life* magazine.

During this time, the political situation in Cuba was changing. General Fulgencio Batista was losing control of Cuba to a new political force headed by Fidel Castro. The leaders of the Batista government were suspicious of everyone, including the famous American author. One night, a government patrol came onto Finca Vigia property searching for weapons. Hemingway's Black Dog began to bark, and he was cruelly killed when a government soldier hit the dog in the head with the butt of his gun. Hemingway was outraged.[3] He could not make an official complaint, because the atmosphere in Cuba was too dangerous. Even though Finca Vigia had been his home for over twenty years, Hemingway knew he could not live in Cuba any longer.

The Hemingways decided to move back to the United States. They settled on an area in the West and rented a house in Ketchum, Idaho, near Sun Valley. Hemingway then bought a two-story chalet, a house with large picture windows and a view of the Sawtooth Mountains and Big Wood River. But before the Hemingways could settle permanently in Idaho, they once again planned another trip abroad.

In his later years, Hemingway wrote a memoir about his life as a young writer in Paris. A Moveable Feast *was not published until after Hemingway's death.*

Hemingway wanted to do more research on bullfighting for his *Life* magazine article.

By spring 1959, Ernest and Mary Hemingway were in Spain, staying at La Consula, a villa owned by a friend named Bill Davis. Mary Hemingway was planning a large surprise party for her husband's sixtieth birthday. While these preparations were going on, Hemingway was busy writing an article he called "The Dangerous Summer." The article, however, kept growing until it had reached more than one hundred thousand words. Eventually, *The Dangerous Summer* became a book on Spain's famous bullfights and the matadors who performed the "Corrida de Toros" (bullfights).

The Hemingways traveled with friends from La Consula to Madrid to follow the bullfights. The trip was exhausting for Mary Hemingway, who came down with a terrible cold. They continued traveling from city to city, following the matadors on their bullfighting circuit. Hemingway seemed to be living at a frantic pace, trying to do all the things he had once done as a young man. Only this time his body and mind were not cooperating. Growing old did not sit well with Hemingway. His son Jack once said that his father "would have made a wonderful old man except that he had never learned to be one."[4]

The trip finally took its toll on Mary Hemingway. She returned to the villa to rest and to finish the preparations for her husband's birthday party. Hemingway, though, was not left alone. He and a group of people made the rounds of the bullfights.

Mary Hemingway's birthday party for her husband

in Spain was a big success largely because of her careful planning. Invited guests from all around the world gathered at La Consula. An orchestra, Flamenco dancers, and fireworks were the highlights of the party. Hemingway appeared to be enjoying himself, but his behavior seemed odd and he was often rude to his wife. It was no secret that Hemingway and his wife did not see eye to eye on many issues. This fourth marriage had been a bumpy one, but in spite of the difficulties, it was in its thirteenth year.

During this time, many of Hemingway's friends had begun to notice his troublesome, unfounded fears. He worried about not having enough money to pay his taxes. He thought the FBI was following him and that there were people who wanted to steal his manuscripts and other possessions. Once, after a friend accidentally touched the back of his head, Hemingway yelled at him, saying that nobody could touch his head.[5]

Back in Cuba, the strange behavior grew worse. Hemingway was working on the bullfighting article and had asked a friend, A. E. Hotchner, to help him with the editing. It was soon obvious to his friend that writing was becoming more difficult for Hemingway. The writer's patience was short, and he was often grumpy. In spite of his condition, he made another trip to Madrid to clear up some details for his *Life* magazine article. He also visited with a friend, the matador Antonio Ordóñez. When Hemingway returned to the home he had bought in Ketchum, Idaho, Mary Hemingway was terribly concerned about his behavior. He seemed to be constantly arguing with her and worrying about his writing.

By November 1960, the Hemingways were living permanently in Ketchum, Idaho. The rugged outdoors that Hemingway loved so much was just a few steps outside his new home. Mountains, woods, and streams welcomed him to his new life. There was plenty of fishing and hunting and lots of time to take long walks through the woods. It was a different environment from his Cuban home. He was no longer near the warm waters of the Gulf Stream or his beloved boat, the *Pilar*. He did not have many servants meeting his daily needs. He also did not have many of the favorite possessions that he had accumulated while living at Finca Vigia. He had left many items behind, unable to transfer all his valuables out of Cuba after Castro's overthrow of the Batista regime.

Writing, which had always comforted him, was now making him anxious. He was trying to finish *A Moveable Feast*, but he was having difficulty finding the right words. He would write and rewrite, spending hours on one sentence. Finally, he gave up on getting the words just right and never finished the ending.

Hemingway's mental condition grew more unstable. On November 30, 1960, he was persuaded to enter the Mayo Clinic in Rochester, Minnesota, under the pretext that he was just going in for a physical examination. It was hoped that once there, he would agree to see a psychiatrist, which he did. His symptoms were treated by electric shock therapy, and he was also taken off some high blood pressure medication that may have contributed to his depression. He returned home at the end of January 1961, eager to return to his writing, which he attempted with great difficulty.

One morning in April, Mary found him in the living room holding a shotgun. She quickly called the doctor, who hurried over and persuaded the writer to give up the gun. Once again, Hemingway was admitted to the Mayo Clinic, but about two months later, on June 26, he was released. Somehow, he had convinced his doctor at the clinic to release him, even though his wife did not feel he was well enough to come home.

During this time, Mary Hemingway had hidden her husband's guns in the cellar, but he managed to find them. In the early morning hours of July 2, 1961, only a few weeks before his sixty-second birthday, Ernest Hemingway died of a self-inflicted gunshot wound to the head. The sound of the gun woke Mary. She found her husband in the front entryway of their Ketchum home. Although Hemingway's death was clearly a suicide, his wife could not acknowledge the truth of what had happened. Initial reports stated that he died in a "hunting accident." In 1966, she finally admitted that her husband had taken his own life.[6]

Hemingway was buried in the small cemetery in Ketchum, Idaho, beneath the towering Sawtooth Mountains. It was a serene setting for a man who had lived a fast-paced, risky, and adventurous life. In the end, his body and mind paid the price for the lifestyle he had chosen. But what a life he had lived!

Hemingway traveled around the world, received fame and fortune from work he loved, married four times, fathered three sons, enjoyed many friends from all walks of life, and had exciting adventures. He accepted the rewards and consequences that were a part of living a full and rich life. He was not a perfect man, son, brother, husband, father, or friend, but he was a gifted and dedicated writer who put all his energies into perfecting his work. In his adventurous lifestyle, his war experiences, and his relationships with women, Hemingway found the inspiration for his writing.

Although Hemingway and his fourth wife did not always get along, he left practically everything in his will to Mary Hemingway, except for a few small bequests. He left his beloved boat, the *Pilar*, to Gregorio Fuentes, his faithful captain of many years. Fuentes never went out in it again, but he did not sell it either. Later, the Cuban government moved the boat to the Finca Vigia property, which Mary Hemingway had donated to the Cuban people. When Hemingway's three sons protested about being left out of the will, Mary Hemingway made provisions for them to receive the income earned from foreign royalties on all their father's books.[7]

Today, Ernest Hemingway's contribution to American literature remains a valued and important part of our literary history. Rising above his celebrity status, lifestyle, human imperfections, and acts of courage and adventure was a man who recognized his own talents, deciding early in life to become a disciplined and dedicated writer. Hemingway wrote in a spare, uncluttered style and was known as a master of dialogue. He brought a new voice to American writing—a clear and powerful prose that he has left behind for new generations of readers and writers to enjoy and reflect upon. This is Ernest Miller Hemingway's true legacy.

Chronology

1899—Ernest Miller is born on July 21 in Oak Park, Illinois.

1917—Graduates from Oak Park High School; goes to work as a reporter for *The Kansas City Star.*

1918—Leaves for overseas duty as a commissioned second lieutenant in the Red Cross; drives an ambulance; injured by a mortar shell; awarded the Italian Medal of Valor; falls in love with a nurse, Agnes von Kurowsky.

1919—Returns to Oak Park as a war hero; lives at home and begins to write seriously; Agnes von Kurowsky breaks off her relationship with Hemingway.

1920—Hemingway's mother tells him he is no longer welcome at their summer home, Windemere; moves to Chicago and stays with friends; meets future wife, Hadley Richardson.

1921—Finds a job in Chicago as a writer and editor for a magazine called *The Cooperative Commonwealth*; marries Richardson on September 3 in Horton Bay, Michigan; Hemingways leave for Paris, France.

1922—While living in Paris, works as a foreign correspondent for the *Toronto Star* newspaper; also works on his own writing.

1923—Publishes his first book, *Three Stories and Ten Poems*; first son, John ("Bumby"), is born in Toronto, Canada.

1924—Returns to Paris; second book, *In Our Time*, is published by Three Mountains Press; later, this book is expanded and published by a New York publisher and is a success in America.

1925—Hemingways follow the bullfights in Pamplona, Spain; begins writing *The Sun Also Rises*.

1926—Two new books, *The Torrents of Spring* and *The Sun Also Rises*, are published by Charles Scribner's Sons.

1927—Publishes a collection of short stories, *Men Without Women*; divorces first wife and marries Pauline Pfeiffer.

1928—Begins work on *A Farewell to Arms*; second son, Patrick, is born; Hemingway's father dies.

1929—*A Farewell to Arms* is published.

1931—Moves to Key West, Florida; third son, Gregory ("Gigi"), is born.

1932—Publishes *Death in the Afternoon*, a book about bullfighting.

1933—*Winner Take Nothing* is published; goes on first African safari with wife Pauline; two of his best short stories come out of this experience: "The Snows of Kilimanjaro" and "The Short Happy Life of Francis Macomber."

1935—*Green Hills of Africa* is published.

1936—Meets Martha Gellhorn.

1937—Publishes *To Have and Have Not*, a novel about the working class versus the rich; reports on the Spanish Civil War.

1938—Publishes a play, *The Fifth Column*.

1940—*For Whom the Bell Tolls* is published; divorces second wife and marries Martha Gellhorn; moves to Cuba.

1941—Hemingway and third wife go to China to cover the Chinese/Japanese War.

1942—During World War II, patrols the Cuban waters on the *Pilar*, searching for German U-boats.

1944—Goes to Europe as a war correspondent for *Collier's*; views the D-day landing on Omaha Beach; is injured in a car accident in London; while covering the war in France, meets Mary Welsh.

1945—Divorces Gellhorn; begins work on a book called *Islands in the Stream.*

1946—Marries Mary Welsh, his fourth wife.

1950—Publishes *Across the River and into the Trees*, his first book in ten years; it is not well received by the critics; begins work on *Garden of Eden.*

1951—His mother dies.

1952—*The Old Man and the Sea* is published; sells five million copies in two days.

1953—Goes on second African safari trip with wife Mary; *The Old Man and the Sea* is awarded the Pulitzer Prize in Literature.

1954—Suffers injuries in two plane crashes; awarded the Nobel Prize for Literature.

1957—Begins work on *A Moveable Feast*, a collection of memories and sketches of his early life in Paris; published in 1964, after his death.

1959—Works on *The Dangerous Summer*, an article on bullfighting that later becomes a book; celebrates his sixtieth birthday at a party given by his wife, Mary.

1960—Leaves Cuba because of political changes; moves to Ketchum, Idaho, near Sun Valley; first suicide attempt; goes to the Mayo Clinic for treatment; *The Dangerous Summer* is published.

1961—Commits suicide on July 2, a few weeks before his sixty-second birthday.

Selected Fiction by Ernest Hemingway

Three Stories and Ten Poems, 1923

In Our Time, 1925

The Torrents of Spring, 1926

The Sun Also Rises, 1926

Men Without Women, 1927

A Farewell to Arms, 1929

Death in the Afternoon, 1932

Winner Take Nothing, 1933

Green Hills of Africa, 1935

To Have and Have Not, 1937

The Fifth Column and the First Forty-Nine Stories, 1938

For Whom the Bell Tolls, 1940

Across the River and into the Trees, 1950

The Old Man and the Sea, 1952

A Moveable Feast, 1964

Islands in the Stream, 1970

The Nick Adams Stories, 1972

The Garden of Eden, 1987

The Complete Short Stories of Ernest Hemingway: The Finca Vigía Edition, 1987

Chapter Notes

Chapter 1. An American Legend

1. Matthew J. Bruccoli, ed., *Conversations With Ernest Hemingway* (Jackson: University Press of Mississippi, 1986), p. 29.

2. Carlos Baker, *Ernest Hemingway: A Life Story* (New York: Charles Scribner's Sons, 1969), p. 486.

3. Ernest Hemingway, *By-Line: Ernest Hemingway*, William White, ed. (New York: Charles Scribner's Sons, 1967), pp. 239–240.

4. Larry Smith, "He Fights for Hemingway," *Parade Magazine*, July 2, 1995, pp. 8–10.

5. Ernest Hemingway, *The Old Man and the Sea* (New York: Simon & Schuster, 1995), p. 103.

6. A. E. Hotchner, *Hemingway and His World* (New York: Vendome Press, 1989), p. 194.

7. Leicester Hemingway, *My Brother, Ernest Hemingway* (Sarasota: Pineapple Press, 1996), p. 14.

Chapter 2. Life in Oak Park, Illinois

1. Kenneth S. Lynn, *Hemingway* (Cambridge: Harvard University Press 1995), p. 42.

2. A. E. Hotchner, *Hemingway and His World* (New York: Vendome Press, 1989), p. 15.

3. Carlos Baker, *Ernest Hemingway: A Life Story* (New York: Charles Scribner's Sons, 1969), p. 17.

4. Cynthia Maziarka and Donald Vogel, Jr., eds. *Hemingway at Oak Park High: The High School Writings of Ernest Hemingway*, 1916–1917 (Oak Park, Ill.: Oak Park and River Forest High School, 1993), p. 94.

5. Ibid., pp. 20–21.

6. Leicester Hemingway, *My Brother, Ernest Hemingway* (Sarasota: Pineapple Press, 1996), pp. 44–45.

Chapter 3. Work, War, and Love

1. Carlos Baker, *Ernest Hemingway: A Life Story* (New York: Charles Scribner's Sons, 1969), pp. 30–31.

2. Kenneth S. Lynn, *Hemingway* (Cambridge: Harvard University Press, 1995), p. 73.

3. Ibid., p. 78.

4. Carlos Baker, *Ernest Hemingway: A Life Story* (New York: Charles Scribner's Sons, 1969), pp. 45–46.

5. Bernice Kert, *The Hemingway Women* (New York: Norton, 1983), p. 58.

6. Ibid., pp. 67–68.

7. Lynn, p. 115.

8. Ibid., pp. 117–118.

9. Baker, p. 72.

Chapter 4. Hadley and Paris

1. Bernice Kert, *The Hemingway Women* (New York: Norton, 1983), pp. 85–86.

2. Gioia Diliberto, *Hadley* (New York: Ticknor and Fields, 1992), p. 70.

3. Ibid., p. 63.

4. Leicester Hemingway, *My Brother, Ernest Hemingway* (Sarasota: Pineapple Press, 1996), p. 73.

5. Ernest Hemingway, *A Moveable Feast* (New York: Macmillan, 1964), p. 12.

6. Ibid., p. 91.

7. Ibid., p. 12.

8. Ibid., title page.

9. Kenneth S. Lynn, *Hemingway* (Cambridge: Harvard University Press 1995), pp. 187–188.

10. Ibid., pp. 219–220.

11. Hemingway, pp. 91–92.

12. A. E. Hotchner, *Hemingway and His World* (New York: Vendome Press, 1989), p. 92.

Chapter 5. Fame, Fortune, and Loss

1. A. E. Hotchner, *Hemingway and His World* (New York: Vendome Press, 1989), p. 10.

2. Bernice Kert, *The Hemingway Women* (New York: Norton, 1983), pp. 217–218.

3. Hotchner, p. 55.

4. Carlos Baker, *Ernest Hemingway: A Life Story* (New York: Charles Scribner's Sons, 1969), p. 199.

5. Ernest Hemingway, *A Farewell to Arms* (New York: Charles Scribner's Sons, 1929), p. 112.

6. Ibid., pp. 184–185.

Chapter 6. A Life of Adventure

1. A. E. Hotchner, *Hemingway and His World* (New York: Vendome Press, 1989), p. 105.

2. Ibid., p. 113.

3. Ibid., p. 139.

4. Ernest Hemingway, epigraph to *For Whom the Bell Tolls* (New York: Charles Scribner's Sons, 1940).

Chapter 7. Papa

1. Larry Smith, "He Fights for Hemingway," *Parade Magazine*, July 2, 1985, p. 10.

2. Norberto Fuentes, *Hemingway in Cuba* (Secaucus, N.J.: Lyle Stuart, 1984), p. 35.

3. Matthew J. Bruccoli, ed., *Conversations With Ernest Hemingway* (Jackson: University Press of Mississippi, 1986), pp. 110–111.

4. A. E. Hotchner, *Hemingway and His World* (New York: Vendome Press, 1989), pp. 154–155.

5. Bernice Kert, *The Hemingway Women* (New York: Norton, 1983), p. 398.

6. Ibid., p. 406.

7. Hotchner, p. 166.

8. Bruccoli, p. 103.

9. Hotchner, p. 178.

Chapter 8. More Adventures

1. Mary Welsh Hemingway, *How It Was* (New York: Knopf, 1976), p. 382.

2. Carlos Baker, *Ernest Hemingway: A Life Story* (New York: Charles Scribner's Sons, 1969), p. 528

3. Mary Welsh Hemingway, p. 412.

4. Baker, p. 529.

Chapter 9. No More Mountains to Climb

1. Carlos Baker, *Ernest Hemingway: A Life Story* (New York: Charles Scribner's Sons, 1969), p. 536.

2. Ibid.

3. Anthony Burgess, *Ernest Hemingway and His World* (New York: Charles Scribner's Sons, 1978), p. 107.

4. Bernice Kert, *The Hemingway Women* (New York: Norton, 1983), p. 487.

5. Baker, p. 548.

6. Kert, p. 505.

7. Jack Hemingway, *Misadventures of a Fly Fisherman: My Life With and Without Papa* (Dallas: Taylor Publishing, 1986), p. 299.

Further Reading

Bruccoli, Matthew J., ed. *Conversations With Ernest Hemingway*. Jackson: University Press of Mississippi, 1986.

Burgess, Anthony. *Ernest Hemingway and His World*. New York: Charles Scribner's Sons, 1978.

Hemingway, Gregory H. *Papa: A Personal Memoir*. Boston: Houghton Mifflin, 1976.

Hemingway, Jack. *Misadventures of a Fly Fisherman: My Life With and Without Papa*. Dallas: Taylor Publishing, 1986.

Hemingway, Leicester. *My Brother, Ernest Hemingway*. Sarasota: Pineapple Press, 1996.

Hotchner, A. E. *Hemingway and His World*. New York: Vendome Press, 1989.

Maziarka, Cynthia, and Donald Vogel, Jr., eds. *Hemingway at Oak Park High: The High School Writings of Ernest Hemingway 1916–1917*. Oak Park, Ill.: Oak Park and River Forest High School, 1993.

Villard, Henry S., and James Nagel. *Hemingway in Love and War: The Lost Diary of Agnes Von Kurowsky*. New York: Hyperion, 1996.

On the Internet

The Ernest Hemingway Museum
<http://204.122.127.50/wshs/oak2.html>

Ernest Hemingway in Oak Park
<http://oprf.com/Hemingway/>

The Papa Page
<http://www.ee.mcgill.ca/~nverever/hem/cover.html>

Index

BALDWIN PUBLIC LIBRARY
3 1115 00429 6454